FACILITATION . . . FROM DISCUSSION TO DECISION

A.L. ZIMMERMAN, Ph.D. & CAROL J. EVANS

NICHOLS PUBLISHING
P.O. Box 6036
East Brunswick, New Jersey 08816
Fax # 908-257-3383

Library of Congress Cataloging-in-Publication Data

Evans, Carol J.
    Facilitation - - from discussion to decision / by Carol J. Evans &
A.L. Zimmerman.
        p.   cm.
    ISBN 0-89397-419-6
    1. Work groups. 2. Group relations training. 3. Leadership.
I. Zimmerman, Anita Louise, 1953 -   .   II. Title.
HD66 . E98   1993   93-4013
658 . 4'036 - - dc20   CIP

DEDICATION

Our work is dedicated to those Facilitators who share our drive, enjoyment, and enthusiasm for the field. We trust this contribution will strengthen their belief in synergy and further their commitment to the discussion process. We applaud their continued accomplishments.

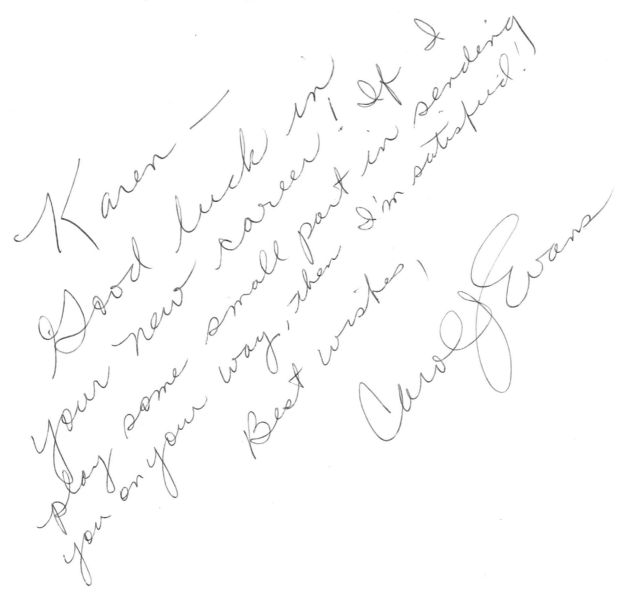

ACKNOWLEDGMENTS

ZIMMERMAN

My Husband - his energy, love, constant support, and unquestioning trust in both the value and the outcome of this process.

My Mother - her love for language, written and spoken, and her respect of its power to influence others.

The Memory of my Father - his unending curiosity and unswerving belief that life and living can always be bettered.

My Brothers - one for his example of sheer determination and progression. One for his example of analytic perfection and thought clarification.

My Assistant - her willingness to review an endless number of revisions, and her patience to work alone much of the time.

And finally, My Writing Partner - her dedication to learning, her flawless desire to share what she understands of the world around her, and above all, her talent for expression.

EVANS

My Husband - provides his unwavering love, laughter, support, and the space to follow my dreams.

My Daughers - fill my life with love, laughter, pride, and challenges.

My Granddaughter - renewed the the child in me. Her curiosity and wonder at all she surveys remind me how precious life is.

My Assistants - their professional and personal support have been a source of strength through the years.

A Special Professor - instigated my return to academe and gave me freedom to pursue my education more fully. The events during that period formed a major turning point in my life.

Finally, My Writing Partner - provided me with many thought provoking hours of ideas, commentary, laughter, and friend-ship. Her enthusiasm and commit-ment made working with her a rich and rewarding experience.

Our Publisher - who believed in our project strongly enough to let us do it "our way."

TABLE OF CONTENTS

i. THE ENTRY
(Introduction)

What exactly comes to mind when you see or hear the word *facilitate?* We have heard the most diverse answers imaginable: From "someone who eases things" to "someone who tells a group what to do." Facilitation is probably the most misunderstood and underused communication and problem-solving tool presently available to management. A primary reason is that a clear definition of the term has not yet been developed.

Traditionally, facilitation was used in psychological counseling environments. Its use in the business arena still bears the brand of that initial purpose. This carryover often includes the myth that Facilitators give no direction, provide no synthesis, and always avoid personal commentary.

To further complicate the issue, many trainers and consultants call themselves "Facilitators" in an effort to appear consistent with today's jargon. Although the title may have changed, the work they perform is essentially the same.

Facilitation is much more than a fad or a trendy label. The term by dictionary definition is "to make less difficult" -- "to make easier." The advantage of such a definition is that it can be used by almost anyone to describe almost anything. The disadvantage is that few people share a common understanding of the term and what it implies. This is not to say that the word *facilitation* should be abandoned. On the contrary, we have only begun to see its emergence as a useful management tool. But a crucial "next step" will be our ability to focus both its meaning and its application.

There are, then, two fundamental questions that need to be answered: 1) What is facilitation? 2) How can it best be used in the business context? This book is designed to provide the groundwork for answers to these questions. The following chapters offer the definition and nature of facilitation, the roles and requirements of Facilitators, and a practical method of matching clients' needs with Facilitators' skills.

I. THE EXPOSURE
(Identification)

Let's look at the word . . . *facilitation*. Once again, the dictionary definition states ". . . to make easier; less difficult." It is ironic that this overly simplistic and somewhat vague definition is used to describe one of the most powerful methods of interaction available to management. Such a generic explanation creates confusion between the expectations of both practitioner and participant.

To discover what facilitation actually means to people and how it is being used, we collected and reviewed a variety of perceptions and definitions. It became clear during our investigation that the implied meaning of facilitate was to "aid the group." The expectation then, is that the Facilitator guides the group through the interaction process step by step.

So far, so good. The real difficulty came when we looked carefully at the uses of facilitation. The ones most commonly reported indicated a definite gap between what was expected and what actually took place. To "make easier" or to "guide" were not the recurring strategies. In fact, no common theme surfaced. Subsequently, we concluded that many of these uses have -- for lack of a better word -- merely been disguised as facilitation.

DELIVERY

In order to support our emerging "Principles of Facilitation," we have classified the most common perceptions and explanations of how facilitation is used. Further, although the individual in each classification is referred to as "Facilitatior," we have renamed their roles to more accurately reflect their actions. The following labels represent the ten most frequently used "Disguises." To help you recognize these, we have provided a description and a warning for each one.

DISGUISES

OBSERVER

Description:

Watches and listens to group interaction, but seldom or never participates. The assumption is that the observer's presence alone will positively affect the group.

Warning:

This presence could be positive or negative. For example, some groups may object to a non-participant's presence. The members may not know or trust why an outsider is there.

JOINER

Description:

Forgoes any semblance of facilitation and blends into the discussion as a member of the group.

Warning:

Objectivity gives an outsider leverage to influence the group. In this disguise group members may no longer see the outsider as being objective. As a result, the potential for leverage may be entirely eliminated.

TRANQUILIZER

Description:

Temporarily diffuses inter-personal conflict, but rarely assists in reaching group goals.

Warning:

The outsider may actually encourage conflict just so the opportunity to neutralize it exists.

HARMONIZER

Description:

Seeks to find peace in every confrontation. The assumption is that <u>any</u> conflict is unhealthy for group interaction.

Warning:

As a result, the group's more dependent members may be intimidated to conform, while its independent members may actually disengage themselves from discussion.

INFORMER

Description:

Passes or disseminates information to the group and sometimes seeks feedback to insure that the message was received.

Warning:

Hidden agendas may be introduced. The outsider is often there to administer predetermined objectives (not necessarily beneficial to the group).

DEALMAKER

Description:

Uses compromise and negotiation to maintain an environment of perpetual dealmaking.

Warning:

The outsider is interested only in the process of making deals rather than reaching group goals -- loves to "deal." Although many agreements are made, the actual outcome may lack relevancy and/or substance.

DIRECTOR

Description:

Initiates actions, controls rather than coordinates group goals. Often tolerates group member interaction rather than genuinely seeking out input.

Warning:

Drives rather than guides the group.

BULLDOZER

Description:

Raw power or fear of exposure is often the motive behind this disguise. The outsider mandates parameters such as choosing the options for discussion and adhering to stringent time lines.

Warning:

Since control must be maintained at all costs, discussion needs strict limitations. The group is propelled to a conclusion, not necessarily a solution.

SORTER

Description:

Selects those group members believed to be most useful or cooperative and defers to them for ideas and input.

Warning:

This bias in selection often leaves the remaining group members to flounder. The excluded members often develop resentment, and will then reposition themselves by becoming either completely withdrawn or overly argumentative.

DIVIDER

Description:

Instigates divisions and provokes disagreements among group members. The outsider aligns and realigns with various members in order to further confuse or weaken the group structure.

Warning:

Although control is maintained, this behavior usually results in a loss of credibility. In addition, it adversely affects the group's productivity and/or life cycle.

These Disguises all claim to be an absolute expression or definition of facilitation. Each one, however, describes a narrowly focused behavior. Although any of the behaviors could be used in a facilitative process, standing alone, any one of them is not facilitation. In other words, by themselves the disguises are inadequate.

There is an additional concern. Since each disguise is believed to be the "whole" of facilitation, those involved often push their roles to an extreme. History tells us that an extreme in almost anything is at best, unhealthy. . . at worst, dangerous. A review of the warnings described above lends support to that historical notion.

In reality, facilitation is not an extreme of any one skill. Rather it is a blend of expertise and skills used to maximize group potential. Facilitators must know when to encourage, when to set boundaries, and when to let the group progress on its own. The challenge then, is the ability to find and maintain this delicate balance.

DIAGNOSES

To better understand the Disguises, it might be useful to ask a few obvious questions about facilitation. What is the goal? How will it be reached? What are the affects?

Looking at overall facilitative strategies has tremendous value when trying to explain goals and objectives. As a result, we returned to our survey and categorized the most obvious strategies into five areas, again with descriptions and warnings. To further clarify why these strategies might be adopted, we have also offered some possible motivations of the Facilitator.

STRATEGIES

INVISIBILITY

Description:

There is comfortability with the group's status quo, and the Facilitator is not distinguishable from the other group members. In addition, a lack of skills and/ or expertise to affect an outcome may result in a fear of maneuvering in unfamiliar territory.

Motivation:

Has a strong desire to be liked.

Warning:
Will not initiate changes. This may result in an inability to take a stand or uphold responsibilities as a Facilitator.

SALVATION

Description:

Does not function effectively in a conflict situation. As a result, conflict is not recognized as a tool for decision making.

Motivation:

Prefers to avoid conflict and, in some cases, even wants to be recognized as a peace-maker.

Warning:
The inability to confront conflict objectively may eliminate it from the group's decision-making process. A reduction in both idea generation and discussion would be the probable result.

CONTROL

Description:

This does not allow participation in leadership or the introduction of new ideas.

Motivation:

Self importance through the preservation of image must be maintained. Sees a loss of control as a sign of weakness. Exposure to vulnerability must be protected at all costs.

MANIPULATION

Description:

The focus centers entirely on the process of interaction, rather than on a balance of process and end result.

Motivation:

Motivations in this category are probably the most widely varied. Some possibilities are money, job security and power (directing the interactions of others). Others just enjoy the challenge of the process. A recognition of who is "in charge" is extremely important.

Warning:
The desire for personal gain may overshadow the productivity of the group's goals. The goals may be entirely sacrificed for the process itself.

INFECTION

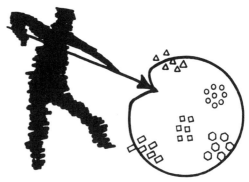

Description:

The Facilitator is a self-styled power broker. Uses and discards group members as needed for self gain.

Motivation:

Seeks to form coalitions to gain support for themselves rather than supporting group goals.

Warning:

May so strongly divide the group that permanent damage results in terms of the group's life cycle. Members who do not "fit" the coalitions are ignored. As a result, stereotypic thinking rather than discussion often becomes the mode of group process.

The observations described above provide possible answers to our original questions.

What is the goal? Perhaps a better question might be: Whose goal is it? There are usually several goals operating simultaneously. The participants, the Facilitator, and the individual who hired the Facilitator all have goals that may or may not be the same. In general, the working goal that can be observed tends to align with the Facilitator's motivations and/or mission.

How will it be reached? Unfortunately, many Facilitators adopt a strategy that helps design disguises. These disguises then become the method or vehicle through which their own goals are accomplished.

What are the effects? There are both individual and group effects from using disguises. From what we have observed and others' reports, we have identified these effects as "Warnings" under both **DISGUISES** (specific) and **STRATEGIES** (general). At best, the effects slow progress, while at their worst they totally disrupt or dissolve the group.

Feelings of frustration and failed expectations are often based on the inaccurate perceptions and opinions of those involved. From our own experiences, these human factors may veil or impede the goal of facilitation by using inappropriate methods. Since our purpose, however, is not just to understand facilitation, but to develop a common language for it, we must move beyond perceptions and into more observable and measurable traits. To do this, we will classify the observable skills that are used as tools by effective facilitators.

DIVISION OF SKILLS

The competent Facilitator utilizes a variety of skills. Interestingly enough, the desired outcomes usually determine how visible any set of skills are at any given time.

INFORMATIVE

The most obvious set of skills includes those used to **inform**.

Depth of knowledge is the primary asset for someone
using these skills.Each skill deals with the interactive
process of transferring that knowledge to the participant(s).

Figure 1.1 INFORMATIVE SKILLS	
Structure	- to develop an agenda and establish the climate.
Direction	- to move or guide toward a goal.
Objectives	- to identify the main steps needed to reach the overall goal.
Feedback	- to respond verbally and nonverbally to participant input.
Focus	- to maintain direction and purpose.
Explanation	- to instruct in or clarify definitions and concepts

Although this is the most common sequence, there is no magic to
the order shown above. The facilitator may choose to apply the
skills independently or in any combination.

INTERPRETIVE

A less obvious, but nonetheless vital, set of skills includes those used to **interpret** concepts and ideas.

Perception is the primary asset for someone using these skills. Each skill requires both a sensitivity to grasp verbal and non-verbal meanings and an ability to organize them into accurate messages.

Figure 1.2   INTERPRETIVE SKILLS

Listening	- to comprehend both the denotative and connotative parts of a message.
Flexibility	- to accept unknowns as assets in goal attainment.
Separation	- to distinguish among issues and provide a logical framework.
Openness	- to acknowledge, understand, and manage emotions.
Process	- to "read" and maintain the flow of interaction.
Translate	- to provide common meanings for definitions and concepts.

The sequence shown above indicates a move from the simplest to the more complex skills. Facilitators usually apply these in a similar order, although the time spent on each skill may vary.

INTUITIVE

The least obvious, but perhaps most crucial set of skills include those that guide **intuition**.

Experience is not just an asset for someone using these skills, it is essential. Since intuition describes primarily intangible abilities, experience is required to know precisely when and exactly where to apply them.

Figure 1.3 INTUTITIVE SKILLS

Create	- to expand the agenda so as to encourage the development of alternative views and sustain an open climate.
Instinct	- to discuss meanings and utilize unknowns by spontaneously combining observation with experience.
Timing	- to select the precise sequence and rate at which concepts are processed for maximum effect.
Empathy	- to identify so completely with the participant(s) that one shares a well as understands their experiences.
Synthesize	- to blend both similar and diverse ideas into understandable concepts.
Integrate	- to skillfully and effectively join separate concepts into a large whole.

It is not necessary to follow the above sequence, but these skills are combined and connected more often than either of the other groupings. In fact, so rarely are they ever seen in isolation that we can say there is a consistent interreliance among them.

Setting the skills side by side, it is apparent why there is so much confusion among both the definitions and the uses of facilitation.

Figure 1.4 COMPANION SKILLS

INFORMATIVE (Knowledgeable)	INTERPRETIVE (Perceptive)	INTUITIVE (Experienced)
Structure	Listening	Create
Direction	Flexibility	Instinct
Objectives	Separation	Timing
Feedback	Openness	Empathy
Focus	Process	Synthesize
Explanation	Translate	Integrate

As one moves from left to right across the chart, it is evident that the skills become both more complex and more challenging to master. A successful Facilitator is able to discern distinctions among meanings and detect the gray areas where those meanings overlap. As the skills become less visible, the ability to recognize (and therefore apply) them, is of particular importance. Without an accepted standard of definition, the task of discernment becomes much more difficult.

CHAPTER SUMMARY

This chapter is an overview of the different ways in which facilitation is perceived. The generic use of the term *facilitation* is discouraged. By providing a common definition we assign it the importance it warrants.

The Disguises and Strategies have been gleaned from both survey and experience. The skill categories begin the process of definition by describing the variety available to the Facilitator. As each skill is chosen or discarded, there is an effect on the participants and ultimately the outcome. These effects will be discussed later in the book.

II. THE EXPLORATION
(Facilitation)

PANORAMA

HISTORICAL BACKGROUND

A backdrop of historical events can provide unexpected insight to the uses and limitations of any skill. Facilitation is no exception. We believe, therefore, it is important to trace the evolution of this tool.

For hundreds and quite likely thousands of years, intervention and interpretation have been used to improve human communication and understanding. These methods forged social contracts among individuals and assisted in the development of trust and respect for one another's viewpoints. Although it may have lacked an official name, clergy, teachers, counselors, psychologists, and a host of other professionals have used this basic tool for centuries. As both a skill and a tool, facilitation's roots are in the helping professions.

Chapter one states that "to facilitate" means "to make easier," and "to guide or help." Needless to say, these are wide parameters for a single tool. In order to narrow the focus into a manageable guideline, we have listed what we consider to be five significant "turning points" in the growth and development of facilitation.

I. **SENSITIVITY**
Increased individual self awareness and greater levels of group trust.

II. **OBJECTIVITY**
Psychology as a legitimate "field of study."

III. **RIGIDITY**
Industry geared to efficient mass production.

IV. **PROFICIENCY**
Human relations needed to maintain production.

V. **TECHNICAL ARTISTRY**
Facilitation as both an art and a science.

The preceding descriptions represent the chronological and perceptual growth of facilitation. Time and time again, it has been at the forefront of idea generation, problem solving, and decision making. If we examine each of these stages in depth, an even clearer picture emerges of the prominent role facilitation has played throughout human history.

Descriptors of each stage along with a series of questions are listed below. The questions will help you determine facilitation's impact on communication during each period.

I. SENSITIVITY

This stage preceded any formal study of human thought or behavior. Those individuals holding positions of high esteem were believed most knowledgeable and capable to deal with anxieties, relational difficulties, and misunderstandings. Clergy were often viewed as pivotal in dispensing human understanding. Others seen as sources for help included teachers, doctors, and to some extent, those representing the law.

At this early stage, facilitation was used primarily to help the individual solve problems, cope with circumstances, and attain greater self awareness. In addition, it was sometimes used to help groups achieve deeper levels of trust and cooperation. Examples of this included family gatherings, town councils, and church meetings.

Whether dealing with an individual or a group, the Facilitator pursued two basic goals. First, the overall aim was to lower the anxiety level of the individual. Second, in the case of group members, the more specific aim was to develop a shared respect for one another's views.

Questions often asked included:

How do you feel?

What do you think?

What do you think they believe?

Do you understand what they are saying?

18

II. OBJECTIVITY

The study of the mind was granted new status during the 1800's when it became an integral part of the scientific community. Psychology began a new phase and its methods were given more serious consideration. This new science was struggling to be recognized as a "legitimate" field of inquiry.

As the variety of "helping" professions increased and psychology gained attention, more and more people were attracted to it as a career. It was soon apparent that these individuals not only needed to develop the skills they already possessed, but should receive exposure to new ones as well. Teachers, for example, expanded their classroom techniques of communication and explanation, while learning the new skills of interpretation and intervention. As a result, much effort was spent studying the tools of psychology and their effective application. Facilitation was one of those skills.

During this period, practitioners were just beginning to seek a framework within which to work. Part of the difficulty in establishing any parameters, however, was that so little was understood about the dynamics of human interaction. Guidelines and structure varied according to professional abilities and personal style.

Questions often asked included:

How do you see yourself as a Facilitator?

How do you see others?

What do you think they really meant by what they said?

How do you determine when, how, and why to apply a specific tool?

III. RIGIDITY

The move from agricultural communities to a manufacturing society brought new problems in human communication. Emphasis on the individual and interpersonal or small group interactions became overshadowed by the Industrial Revolution and a sharp rise in immigration. As a result of these forces, two major changes occurred in the work environment. The number and diversity of people working together increased, and the location of the workplace shifted.

Traditionally, those working side by side were family members or well-known neighbors. With this new industrial society, however, strangers worked together. Instead of a single homogeneous group, members from various groups were forced to work closely in what was now to all of them a "foreign environment." To further complicate the situation, individuals were no longer able to exercise their own methods of working. In this system, how, when, and where to work was decided for them.

The resulting loss of autonomy brought an unfamiliar rigidity to the concept of "work." Resentment and uncertainty emerged as workers tried to cope with their new "workplace." One of the most difficult problems facing employees and management alike was how to communicate and cooperate with those you did not know, but who powerfully impacted your own productivity.

Questions often asked included:

How can we achieve the goal?

Do we understand the goals?

How many groups do we need?

How closely should we cooperate?

IV. PROFICIENCY

Concern for human interactions and relationships have been temporarily displaced by the drive for mass production and urban living. There were simply too many people to maintain the traditional types of one-on-one interactions. Quantity and rate of production became the primary goals for most organizations.

Ultimately, however, efficiency was no longer sufficient to maintain or achieve high production. The resentment and uncertainty felt by workers affected their motivation and consequently, their output. Increasing demands for production and an ever-growing number of employees highlighted a need for the "human component." Further, there was a realization of the necessity for the systematic study of behavior in the workplace.

As a result, the study of individuals expanded to include the study of collective groups. This area was soon termed "organizational dynamics" and/or "organizational development" in the work environment. This new emphasis began to unfold about the same time psychology was gaining scientific legitimacy and commercial popularity. Only a short time elapsed before these two disciplines connected and slowly began to interweave. The eventual marriage of psychology and organizational dynamics was undeniably necessary for the advancement of human systems.

Organizations are humans. As such, they are the result of collective human thought and action. To understand how these systems operate and how they may be improved, we need to understand the mind and how it interacts with others. The relatively new science of psychology was a ready source for an explanation of human thought and behavior. In fact, a primary technique of psychotherapy was found to have equal success when applied to the study of organizational behavior. This technique was facilitation.

The emphasis in facilitation training, therefore, was in the areas of group discussion, group process, process consultation, and group problem solving. Facilitators were essentially viewed as guides or directors of these encounters. In the literature of psychotherapy, they were referred to as "leaders" (see Yalom, 1975, and Hansen, Warner, and Smith, 1976).

Although little was done to coordinate any shared definition of the term "facilitation," there was no question that it had been accepted as a viable tool. Its widespread use without a frame of reference, however, created confusion among practitioners and participants alike.

Questions often asked included:

How can your group best achieve its goal?

How do you best function in your community or civic groups?

What are more effective ways of communicating with others in your work group?

What abilities must Facilitators possess to excel at any one technique?

How do Facilitators determine when, how, and why to apply a specific technique?

V. TECHNICAL ARTISTRY

The most recent change of emphasis could be classified more accurately as a transition rather than a true change or alteration. Facilitation is now used more often and applied to more circumstances than possibly any other tool of human interaction. Such pervasive application gives it increasing credibility in both personal and organizational life. Credibility mixed with popularity has provided facilitation a unique position in the organizational behavior toolbox. It is, in fact, found in a variety of toolboxes across a diversity of professions.

There is currently a desire among many Facilitators to consolidate or define this multi-dimensional, multi-disciplinary tool. Systematic studies are beginning to analyze the use of Facilitators and their effect on the group process and problem solving. Individual institutions, universities, consulting firms, and organizations are trying to establish their own skill requirements for Facilitators. At present, however, there has been no consensus as to the scope, use or even nature of facilitation.

One unified perception that <u>has</u> evolved is that facilitation is far more complex than we had once thought. There are fundamental skills that can be taught to "certify" one as a Facilitator. Yet skills alone are not sufficient. Effective Facilitators appear to possess an insight that is beyond the learning of a technique. There is an observable "artistry" in facilitation. Today, greater energy is focused on the need for balance between knowledge and application; between facilitation as a skill, and facilitation as an art.

Questions often asked included:

What are the areas of natural talent and abilities of workers?

How much commitment is behind their agreement?

Do we actually make <u>contact</u> when we communicate?

How can we improve decision making?

How small is our "global village"?

23

Summary

These stages mark the major turning points in the use of facilitation. A quick scan confirms that the technique was widely used long before it was actually understood.

As society grew, so did the demand for improved methods of group interaction. Facilitation was easily accessible and equally adept in varied environments. Continued and more frequent use of the technique brought a recognition of its power and impact on the group process.

The practice of facilitation evolved to accommodate the historical pressures of population, production, and cooperation. This evolution was also marked by the types of questions asked during each stage. The wording of each question became progressively global, more inclusive, with more of the "we," less of the "me." Its present use has gained more attention and stature than perhaps any other single communication or management tool.

MATRIX

The historical perspective demonstrates the changing nature and what could be described as "fluid" parameters of facilitation. Since there is still no agreed-on definition, other methods are often used in place of or in conjunction with this technique. In this section, we will define facilitation and its two counterparts: Training and Consulting.

These counterparts were identified because they normally are accepted as two distinct professions, each of which uses facilitation as desired. We have separated the three in order to establish facilitation as its own field. Its characteristics are unique and not fully interchangeable with training and consulting. To help visualize the relationship among these three areas, we will present a matrix that identifies, compares and contrasts their dominant characteristics.

DEFINITIONS

Training provides information concerning skills and/or knowledge. It offers new understanding, initiates new skills competency, or further develops skills the participants already possess.

Consulting provides analysis, suggestions, options, and/or alternatives. It offers an opportunity to develop ideas and explore solutions.

Facilitating provides a method of adjusting and regulating interaction. It offers an environment conducive to flexible and creative decision making.

From our observations, it is apparent to us that there exists very real differences among these areas. After closely examining our notes, we have chosen the primary characteristics we believe describe the distinct qualities of Trainers, Consultants and Facilitators. These fundamental characteristics have been arranged in a matrix and may be used as a visual chart of comparison.

Figure 2.1 COMPARISON MATRIX			
Contingencies	**Trainers**	**Consultants**	**Facilitators**
Nature:	Resource	Problem Solver	Catalyst
Purpose:	Transfer of knowledge	Provide direction for problem resolution	Assist in intragroup communication
Role:	Instructor	Adviser	Translator
Method:	Present	Propose	Guide
Quality:	Knowledge	Experience	Objectivity
Impact:	Individual	Individual or Group	Dyad or Group
Scope:	Small to Large Groups	Individual/ Small Groups	Small/ Medium Groups

As in any rendering of a dynamic process, there are no absolute boundaries among these descriptions. The words or phrases used in the matrix represent the most prominent characteristics and most apparent tendencies of each function. We have listed below the seven major contingencies, their functional descriptors, and examples of how these traits can occasionally overlap.

1. Nature

What is the essence of each function?

Trainers	- These individuals possess and can access information in a variety of areas.
Consultants	- They are usually viewed as problem solvers. Consultants do access information, but are better known for their ability to manipulate it.
Facilitators	- They stimulate actions and reactions during the communication process.

2. Purpose

What is their primary intent?

Trainers	- They educate participants in skills, information, and competencies.
Consultants	- They identify, order, and analyze issues.
Facilitators	- They foster a full examination and discussion of group issues, and promote participant involvement.

3. Role

What is their observable behavior?

Trainers	- They are seen to provide outlines and formats of prepared information.
Consultants	- They are seen by others to suggest or offer solutions for particular problems or areas of concern.
Facilitators	- They are seen by others to synthesize and often reword or rephrase participant comments.

4. Method

What is their fundamental technique?

Trainers	- They deliver primarily by oral and visual means their understanding of the information.
Consultants	- They recommend ideas, alternatives, or plans of action for consideration.
Facilitators	- They navigate group interaction through a complex network of cooperation, confrontation, and compromise.

5. Quality

What is their predominant attribute?

Trainers	- They have developed an expertise and are able to convey information in specified subject areas.
Consultants	- They have acquired a practical wisdom from applying their education through personal observation and participation.
Facilitators	- They use their judgment, insight, and seasoned abilities to cultivate an unbiased and impartial environment for the group interaction process.

28

6. Impact

Who do they most influence?

Trainers	- Although most training is presented in group settings, the goal is for individual advancement.
Consultants	- Goals and circumstances vary with each situation. As a result, targeted audiences may be either individuals or groups.
Facilitators	- Although they may occasionally guide the decision making of an individual, emphasis is on the interaction process of two or more.

7. Scope

What is the group size involved?

Trainers	- They may address any number of people limited only by the physical constraints of message delivery and audience participation. Trainers adjust their tools and techniques to accommodate the particular demand.
Consultants	- Earlier interactions generally involve only one or two people. Although the number involved may eventually increase, limited size allows for a clearer exchange of information and perspective.
Facilitators	- They normally work with a limited number of people. In general, the larger the group, the more difficult it is to listen, regulate, and synthesize meaningful interaction.

29

The intent of the matrix is not to limit or restrict an individual. Rather, its purpose is to identify the minimal capabilities required for each of the three functions. Skills and capabilities, however, are not the only considerations of facilitation. There are many perceptions operating before, during, and after the sessions.

PERCEPTION

In any facilitative situation, there are three distinct roles; the Producer (the one who hires or chooses Facilitators), the Participant (usually an employee), and the Provider (the Facilitator). Each role carries its own perceptions about the process.

Over the years, we have heard and recorded dozens of perceptions. In the following section we have identified and arranged the most common of these into three categories -- motivations, expectations, and responsibilities for each role. Finally, the categories are further organized into two groupings -- those considered realistic, and those considered unrealistic.

TRY CHECKING YOUR OWN PERCEPTIONS AND EXPERIENCES AGAINST THOSE LISTED.

MOTIVATIONS
(Realistic)

Producer

1. Develop employees' communication and decision-making skills.

2. Increase participant involvement through a forum for open discussion.

3. Initiate and/or advance team development.

4. Examine issues and explore alternatives.

5. Encourage brainstorming and productive problem solving.

Participant

1. Participate in the growth and development of the company.

2. Develop as a team member and contribute to cooperation within and among groups.

3. Gain new perspectives, views, and information.

4. Share insights, opinions, and expertise.

5. Exercise and demonstrate creative and analytic skills.

Provider

1. Participate in the progress of positive group functioning.

2. Offer an objective framework.

3. Foster and enhance participation.

4. Provide focus for multiple and diverse inputs.

5. Explore all possible scenerios.

EXPECTATIONS
(Realistic)

Producer

1. Process will stimulate group participation.

2. Facilitator possesses a broad knowledge base and will provide an objective viewpoint.

3. Degree of understanding team development will increase.

4. Sharing of ideas, concerns and plans will require time.

5. Outcomes may differ from what was initially anticipated.

Participant

1. Forum exists in which to express diverse views.

2. Facilitator is as impartial and objective as possible.

3. Opportunity is present to exercise persuasion.

4. Conflicts, both intrapersonal (within an individual) and interpersonal (between and among individuals), may occur.

5. Process of group discussion requires time.

Provider

1. Facilitator is supplied with sufficient background information and given freedom to coordinate the process.

2. Producer is committed to the process, and understands the range of possible outcomes.

3. Participants have been instructed on the reasons for and importance of the sessions.

4. Conflict should be anticipated and explored as a natural part of the discussion process.

5. Without guidance, participants may not use the appropriate tools and techniques for group discussion.

RESPONSIBILITIES
(Realistic)

Producer

1. Understand and support the total commitment required (time, money, priorities).

2. Give all necessary or connected information to the Facilitator concerning the organization, group members, and the relevant issues.

3. Clarify the procedure, expectations and possible outcomes with the Facilitator.

4. Inform all participants of their role in the process.

5. Demonstrate trust in the Facilitator's ability to guide the group.

Participant

1. Participate fully in the process (preparedness as well as session participation).

2. Take an active role in the discussion process; such as asking for clarification, drawing out quiet or reluctant members, and sharing expertise as needed.

3. Understand and accept the principles of process training.

4. Willingness to be flexible and open-minded.

5. Demonstrate trust in the group process and a commitment to any of its outcomes.

Provider

1. Remain impartial throughout the process by providing objective questions and statements.

2. Change format and direction as needed to maintain open discussion.

3. Provide group with a framework and sufficient guidelines for effective processing.

4. Synthesize and summarize inputs for maximum effectiveness and buy in.

5. Build as much trust as is possible between and among group members.

MOTIVATIONS
(Unrealistic)

Producer

1. Confidential information can and will be disclosed.

2. Process may be used to separate, embarrass, or alienate participants.

3. Manipulation of decision making is sanctioned.

4. Group will be lead to a predetermined outcome.

5. Using facilitation once is sufficient for maximum group effectiveness.

Participant

1. Attend the sessions in order to keep my job.

2. Dominate the discussion through my particular expertise.

3. Use forum only for negative criticism.

4. Block the development of creative alternatives.

5. Disrupt the process to weaken its credibility.

Provider

1. Preservation of my ego and self image supersedes group needs.

2. Control the group members and their interactions.

3. Manipulate the group process toward predetermined goals.

4. Maintain harmony at all costs.

5. Fulfill a desire to be liked.

EXPECTATIONS
(Unrealistic)

Producer

1. Decisions will always be reached, and closure attained.

2. Harbor hidden agendas and/or expectations never discussed with the Facilitator.

3. Everyone will become a team player and demonstrate buy in.

4. Facilitation will provide immediate solutions to all problems.

5. Facilitation sessions will automatically provide full cohesiveness and cooperation.

Participant

1. All of my ideas will be accepted and used.

2. Process is not nearly as important as implementation.

3. Closure should occur with every issue and at the close of every session.

4. Outcomes have been planned in advance.

5. Any implementation should be immediate.

Provider

1. Participants understand their own and the Facilitator's roles and responsibilities in the process.

2. Groups are always eager to work with the Facilitator.

3. Enthusiasm is a sign that the group understands and accepts the process.

4. Group members are always willing to work with one another.

5. Groups will follow each of my process suggestions.

RESPONSIBILITIES
(Unrealistic)

Producer

1. Distinguishing among Trainers, Consultants and Facilitators is not important.

2. Hiring the Facilitator was my final responsibility.

3. There is a need and/or desire to direct sessions myself.

4. Showing impatience to the process is not damaging to the group.

5. Following facilitation, participants should fully trust me and my decisions.

Participant

1. My full participation is unnecessary.

2. One contribution per session fulfills my obligation.

3. Situations that don't directly affect me are not my concern.

4. Discussions should be realigned to accommodate my concept of organization.

5. Reaching closure means making a decision to implement.

Provider

1. Producer's preconceived expectations must be met at all costs.

2. Control of the group and its outcome is primary.

3. All members will come to like, trust, and respect one another.

4. Discussion process must be kept harmonious at all times.

5. Groups must reach their concept of closure.

As simple and seemingly obvious as they appear, these perceptions may well determine the recognized success or failure of facilitation. When Motivations, Expectations, and Responsibilities move in dissimilar directions, they dramatically affect the outcomes of the process. It is important, therefore, that all those involved with facilitative sessions understand the tendencies for unrealistic perceptions to dominate their thinking. It is particularly crucial for facilitators to recognize such inclinations. The acceptance of this phenomenon will encourage preventive measures and allow for more productive sessions.

CHAPTER SUMMARY

This chapter began with an historical overview of the evolution of facilitation. The five developmental stages show the growth and utilization of the tool.

To further identify facilitation as an independent field, we have presented a descriptive matrix. The chart compares and contrasts characteristics of Training, Consulting, and Facilitating.

Following the matrix is an inventory of the most common realistic and unrealistic Motivations, Expectations, and Responsibilities held by all those involved in the facilitation process. Emphasis is placed on the recognition, understanding and proper alignment of these perceptions.

III. THE ENVIRONMENT
(Task)

PURPOSE

<u>WHY FACILITATION/FACILITATORS?</u>

We have defined facilitation as ". . . a method of adjusting and regulating interaction." Fundamentally, the facilitation process moves a general discussion to a more focused, goal-oriented one. It stimulates communication, encourages the examination of ideas and discussion, and promotes Participant involvement.

The creation and maintenance of a conducive environment is essential for productive facilitation. The conditions that surround Participants directly affect their perceptions and consequently, their outcomes. As a result, the environment must be psychologically and physically flexible, and as free of bias and partiality as possible.

The need to sustain a "conducive" environment, then, is the primary reason to seek a Facilitator. Facilitators constantly scan the surroundings and use their observation and experience to properly balance the human and physical dynamics. They are translators of ideas and monitors of emotion, and act as guides through the challenging labyrinth of conflict and resolution.

Facilitators must be able to push, pull, release, encourage, create, and dispel as needed. They need to focus energy without drawing attention to themselves, and rephrase concepts without altering their meanings. The demands placed on these individuals are difficult and at times, risky. It is, therefore, crucial that chosen Facilitators have a seasoned blend of technical skills and intuitive insight.

MATCHING EXPECTATIONS/GOALS

Although the reasons for using facilitation are varied and complex, they all include a common theme. That commonality is the need to match expectations and goals across the three roles involved: **Producer, Participant, and Provider (Facilitator).**

The first step toward alignment is an agreement on terminology. There are at least seven commonly used labels to describe the elements of facilitation.

Figure 3.1 FACILITATION TERMINOLOGY

Expectations	- preconceived realistic and unrealistic assumptions.
Goals	- agreed directions and desired targets.
Commitment	- a binding obligation by all three roles to provide the resources needed for the process (such as time, energy, money, and facilities).
Trust	- a belief and/or feeling of security and confidence that allows for open/candid discussion.
Process	- a series of progressive steps used to address, discuss, and resolve issues.
Responsibility	- individual acceptance of accountability to the process and each other.
Effect	- an intentional or unintentional result of individual, group or organizational effort.
Outcome	- an actual consequence of interaction or behavior.

It is insufficient, however, for those involved merely to understand and adopt the above terms. True facilitation is dependent on the ability of Producers, Participants, and Providers (Facilitators) to successfully align these meanings with their implications.

Figure 3.2 ASSESSMENT OF INDIVIDUAL GOALS AND EXPECTATIONS

LEVEL	INDIVIDUAL		GROUP		ORGANIZATION	
DIRECTION	SELF DEVELOPMENT	CAREER PLANNING	TEAM DEVELOPMENT	POSITIONING	CHANGE	GROWTH
RANGE PROCESS (Short Term)						
HELP						
HINDER						
EXTENDED (Long Term)						
HELP						
HINDER						

40

The "Level" clarifies individuals' perceptions of themselves and others. "Direction" describes general categories by which comments may be sorted. These are not intended to be exclusive, but do represent six of the most common "whys" for pursuing a goal. Finally, the "Range" indicates the time frame involved.

Identified goals from the "Direction" section are subsequently categorized as either short term (process) or long term (extended). Of course, some goals may fit into both time frames. In addition, the chart allows an observer to distinguish these goals as a help or a hindrance. There is also the possibility that some goals may both help and hinder the process. This section then, most directly concerns the Facilitator.

Process goals are short term implications that have an immediate impact on facilitated sessions. It is impractical to expect identical process goals from each individual. Nevertheless, sharp contrasts can impede, corrode, or even destroy the overall process. It is crucial, therefore, that there be a compatible alignment of process goals among all those involved.

Extended goals are longer-term implications and may have no definable time limit. As always, the ideal is to reach a close or complementary alignment of goals among the individuals. Sessions held immediately, however, will not likely be affected by this group of goals. Instead, a more critical focus should be directed toward the shorter term (process) area.

The chart also offers optional uses. First, the goals within each of the six classifications may be prioritized and dealt with accordingly. Second, the chart is designed for use with an individual, but can be adapted easily to group use. As an example, members of a department, division, or organization may be identified as a "single" unit. Third, it is also possible to compare different vantage points on the same chart: An individual's self awareness; the group's perceptions of its own goals; and the organization's view of itself.

Overall, the assessment chart is non-invasive and provides distinct advantages for the Facilitator:

1. Information can be more efficiently separated and prioritized.

2. Comments can be quickly summarized and noted during or after interviews.

3. Diverse goals can be contrasted and compared with greater ease.

4. Common categories allow for continuity of translation and analysis by other facilitators involved in the process.

PREPARATION

The responsibility for preparing a "conducive" environment rests with both the Facilitator and the Producer. Many aspects of this preparation are readily apparent and even anticipated by the Producer. These include: Dates, time, location, travel, lodging, breaks, and room layout. Facilitators usually make suggestions for these logistics, along with specific, routine requirements of their own. As important as these aspects are, however, they comprise only a small portion of preparation.

There is a much larger area that is not so easily recognized or clearly defined. It is absolutely essential that Facilitators help Producers identify these vital yet often invisible elements. Of all the intangibles, trust and commitment are the most critical for constructing a solid foundation.

TRUST

Trust is, in and of itself, a process. It evolves through constant nurturing and rigorous application. It is like mortar, helping to keep the group intact during the most difficult phases of facilitation. Trust in the facilitation process, the Facilitator, and in themselves is required by everyone involved.

Participants' trust in the process assumes a working knowledge of the underlying premise of facilitation. They need to exercise a belief that active participation increases understanding, and raises the odds of an effective resolution. As a result, patience and tolerance must be practiced during periods of sharing, interaction, and conflict.

Facilitators should be trusted for their skill, sensitivity and ability to retain the overall objective. Many Participants or Producers who "dislike" a Facilitator are instead disagreeing with the techniques, the timing, or the direction of the outcome. Criticisms should be examined against skill and experience levels. In addition, Participants are not normally part of the initial planning process where goals and objectives are set. Some may even be working from their own agendas. Their comments and behaviors, therefore, should be assessed to insure accuracy, validity, and attention to purpose.

Further, one primary reason to hire a Facilitator is to have a skilled, objective outsider actively question, challenge and focus the group. Oftentimes, Participants are impatient and push for closure, sometimes to the exclusion of process. This not only hampers the Facilitator's flexibility, but can severely limit or extinguish productive interaction.

Finally, Participants must trust themselves. The facilitation process will provide them an opportunity to sharpen perceptions and develop creativity. They must be willing, however, to become vulnerable, and act and respond with openness and candor. Beyond this, they must trust one another. Respect must be exchanged to foster a bonding in purpose and cooperation.

As gains are made in process understanding and acceptance, a communication bridge may then be built to encourage trust among all involved. True, long-term trust will develop slowly through a series of useful interactions and behaviors. Acknowledgment of one another's feelings and respect for one another's thoughts is the basis for progressive communication. Such an ongoing dialogue, in turn, promotes both personal growth and the process as a whole.

COMMITMENT

Every Facilitator knows there is superficial (or "lipservice") commitment, and there is genuine, deep-seated commitment. A key component of preparation is the ability to distinguish between the two.

Superficial commitment is by far the most frequently demonstrated. These individuals declare their commitment to the outcomes, but rarely show true dedication to the process. They are generally helpful and courteous, yet lack an understanding of the full impact and implications of participative involvement. It is often assumed, however, that anyone having this type of commitment is at heart, uncaring, uninvolved, and/or hostile toward the process. Although there are indeed individuals who possess such an unproductive attitude, there are others who simply do not understand the meaning or expression of genuine commitment. They may, in fact, believe that they are committed, without having a realistic idea of what is actually expected of them.

Since these motives differ so dramatically, the Facilitator's coping mechanisms must adjust accordingly. An unproductive attitude usually demands some type of confrontation, while a lack of understanding generally necessitates education. The former requires a reduction or elimination of barriers, while the latter builds on an enlargement or enrichment of knowledge. Of course, most cases require a blending or mixing of coping mechanisms. This is particularly true when varying levels of commitment are identified within the same management team.

Genuine commitment is a true delight to both watch and experience. As stated above, however, it can be quite difficult to identify. As an example, many Facilitators mistake enthusiasm for commitment. It is commonplace that clients initially appear enthusiastic about a process they believe will help them. The difference between their enthusiasm and genuine commitment is what could best be described as an abyss of disillusionment. As unrealistic motivations, expectations, and responsibilities are replaced with realistic counterparts, their enthusiasm often wanes, and with it, their alleged commitment.

When there is true commitment to facilitation, there is both an understanding and acceptance of the true aspects of the process. Realistic motivations, expectations, and responsibilities address individual and group needs while acknowledging physical and psychological limitations. Genuine deep-seated commitment allows for human and environmental variances, unexpected outcomes, and total participation.

PROCESS GUIDELINES

One way to validate trust and commitment is to formally establish them through a set of process guidelines. There are concrete steps the Facilitator can take to help establish a shared purpose and provide a common structure. A checklist and orientation tools have been developed to lend continuity and order to the process. They are presented in a progressive sequence (Before, During, and After) to demonstrate the complexity of facilitation.

Before

"Why" we do something is important. Without the "why," we have no direction and little or no motivation to move forward. Although it is impossible to anticipate every contingency, orientation tools can provide definition, direction, and at least initial momentum.

Before the session occurs, there are three informational guides that should be distributed. These tools are designed to introduce and promote the process. They are meant to dispel misconceptions and confusion, and eliminate or soften communication barriers. The "Reference Guide on Facilitation" is intended for both the Participant and Producer. It clarifies the purpose of the process and the role of the Facilitator. Two additional tools are for the Participant and the Producer respectively, and establish realistic expectations and responsibilities for their roles (normally the Producer receives a copy of each).

45

Figure 3.3 REFERENCE GUIDE ON FACILITATION

WHAT IS FACILITATION?

Facilitation is used to focus discussion toward a desired goal.

There is no one approach to facilitation.

The goal itself may range from expanding discussions to reaching decisions.

Facilitation:

- Is a method for the exchange of ideas.

- Develops and clarifies the interaction process.

- Acts as a forum for differing views and perspectives.

- Is used to challenge and stretch thinking patterns.

- Encourages a thorough questioning of assumptions.

- Provides an opportunity for exploration and the generation of alternatives.

- Helps to merge and classify thoughts.

WHY USE A FACILITATOR?

Cultivates an unbiased and impartial environment for interaction.

Assures a full examination and discussion of issues.

Provides an objective framework.

Maintains focus so that purposeful discussion does not deteriorate to merely casual conversation.

Offers a method for organizing diverse and multiple viewpoints.

Regulates interaction to allow all those involved access to the process.

Diffuses destructive behaviors and unproductive conflict.

Supplies a visual and verbal tracking of ideas.

Facilitator acts as a:

- Translator by rewording or rephrasing comments without altering the meanings.

- Guide or navigator through the process of cooperation, confrontation, and compromise.

- Point of stability during periods of misunderstanding or conflict.

- Monitor of emotions.

Figure 3.4 PRODUCER ORIENTATION

EXPECTATIONS - REALISTIC

1. Develop employees' communication and decision-making skills.
2. Increase Participant involvement through a forum for open discussion.
3. Advance and/or initiate team development.
4. Examine issues and explore alternatives.
5. Encourage brainstorming and productive problem solving.
6. Process will stimulate group participation.
7. Facilitator will provide an objective viewpoint.
8. Degree of understanding team development will increase.
9. Sharing of ideas, concerns, and plans will require time.
10. Outcomes may differ from what was initially anticipated.
11. Session outcomes are excellent tools for learning more about the people within the organization.

EXPECTATIONS - UNREALISTIC

1. Decisions will be reached, and closure attained.
2. Everyone will become a team player and demonstrate buy in.
3. Facilitation will provide immediate solutions to problems.
4. Facilitation sessions will automatically result in cohesiveness and cooperation.
5. Disclosures will always be forthcoming and candid.
6. Group will be lead to a predetermined outcome.

RESPONSIBILITIES - REALISTIC

1. Understand and support the nature of commitments required (especially time requirements).
2. Give necessary or connected information to the Facilitator concerning the organization, group members, and the relevant issues.
3. Inform Participants of their role in the process.
4. Utilize a receptive rather than critical perspective to review session information and outcomes.

RESPONSIBILITIES - UNREALISTIC

1. Once the Facilitator is hired, there is no need to assume any further responsibility for the process.
2. Providing background information is only necessary in extreme situations.
3. Most Participants require little explanation or encouragement from me for their full involvement.

47

Figure 3.5 PARTICIPANT ORIENTATION

EXPECTATIONS - REALISTIC

1. Participate in the growth and development of the organization.
2. Develop as a team member and contribute to cooperation within and among groups.
3. Gain new perspectives, views, and information.
4. Share insights, opinions, and expertise.
5. Exercise and demonstrate creative and analytic skills.
6. Forum exists in which to express diverse views.
7. Facilitator is as impartial and objective as possible.
8. Opportunity is present to exercise persuasion.
9. Conflicts, both intrapersonal (within oneself) and interpersonal (between and among individuals), may occur and are a natural part of creative problem solving.
10. The process of group discussion requires time.
11. The process will go beyond the dissemination of information that occurs at "routine" meetings.
12. Outcomes may differ from what was initially anticipated.

EXPECTATIONS - UNREALISTIC

1. All of my ideas will be accepted and used.
2. Process is not nearly as important as implementation.
3. Closure should occur with every issue and at the close of every session.
4. Any implementation should be immediate.
5. Outcomes have been planned in advance.
6. Forum merely exists to voice general frustrations and complaints, without any real attempt to problem solve.

RESPONSIBILITIES - REALISTIC

1. Participate fully in the process (preparedness as well as session participation).
2. Take an active role in the discussion process; such as, asking for clarification, drawing out quiet or reluctant members, and sharing expertise as needed.
3. Willingness to be flexible and open-minded.
4. Demonstrate trust in the group process and a commitment to its outcomes.
5. Make accessible or have ready any relevant information.

RESPONSIBILITIES - UNREALISTIC

1. Full participation is unnecessary.
2. Situations that don't directly affect me are not my concern.
3. Discussions should conform to my concept of organization and progress.
4. Reaching closure means making a decision to implement.

There are also Optional Tools that the Facilitator may use. Two of the most productive are Interviews and Focus Instruments. One is usually used to the exclusion of the other, and of the two, interviews are perhaps the optimal choice.

Private face-to-face dialogue between the Facilitator and each Participant can reveal motivations, apprehensions, attitudes, hidden agendas, expectations, and communicative styles. From this information, the Facilitator can identify trends and further analyze the degree of goal alignment. Participants, however, may not be geographically available. In addition, interviews are added hourly charges, and as a result, may be cost prohibitive for some clients.

An alternative to interviews is the use of a Focus Instrument. The instrument is designed utilizing information previously collected from the Producer (projected goals, organizational charts, issues, sample minutes, stated mission, and so on). The Facilitator writes a brief survey questionnaire relating to the proposed issues. It is distributed to all Participants for completion and return prior to the session. These responses can provide individual and group readings similar to those gleaned from interviews. Although not as desirable as one-on-one, Focus Instruments are an effective substitute when time or money is a consideration.

During

As the session begins, there are additional steps that can be taken to prepare the Participants, bringing everyone to a similar starting point. Using a backdrop of orientation tools, the Facilitator can emphasize concrete behaviors and issues that deal directly and specifically with the interaction process.

First and probably foremost is the need to establish a base line regard for one another. So important is this need, a written *Rights of Respect* should be given to each member. It seeks to explain the differences between nonproductive conflict, and the creative challenge of ideas and attitudes.

The guideline is meant not only to provide boundaries of behavior, but is also intended to heighten the awareness of all Participants to potential abuses. Insensitivity could significantly slow or even shut down the sharing and development of ideas. These *Rights of Respect* attempt to demonstrate the vulnerability involved in the process and how sensitive one must be to all verbal and nonverbal communication signals.

Figure 3.6 RIGHTS OF RESPECT

Challenging an idea presented promotes discussion.

> Personal verbal attacks destroy confidence.

Sharing the floor creates an opportunity for understanding.

> Hoarding the speaking "floor" holds the process prisoner.

Sensitivity to others' comments and reactions is necessary for effective interaction.

> Interpreting comments too personally can lead to defensiveness.

Participants should be encouraged to develop and build on others' ideas.

> Believing that ideas are complete as stated stifles creativity and limits outcomes.

The role of Devil's Advocate is an important tool for clarifying and expanding ideas.

> Taking a position on an issue just for the sake of argument is nonproductive.

Comments often need rewording or extending with examples to help others understand.

> Refusal or reluctance to acknowledge participants' confusion or uncertainty undermines trust and shared vulnerability.

Good listening skills demonstrate avid participation and a willingness to consider other viewpoints.

> Distractions or side conversations break group concentration, and show both a lack of interest and respect for other Participants.

Second, verbal "highlights" of the previously distributed Participant Orientation Tool should be presented. This should force an awareness of the most critical aspects of the process. Following is a suggested list of highlights. (Corresponding references to the Expectation section of the Participant Orientation Tool are indicated by number and category.)

Facilitator Role

- Impartial and objective.
- Acts as a translator.
- Not a critic.
- Often challenges and questions Participants for clarification.
(#7 Realistic Expectations)

Persuasion

- Atmosphere is relatively non threatening.
- Is encouraged and expected among Participants.
- Demands a thinking through of reason and outcomes.
(#8 Realistic Expectations)

Conflict

- Should be anticipated.
- Is a natural consequence of idea exchange.
- Is necessary for any type of creativity.
(#9 Realistic Expectations)

Exchange

- Is not just information dissemination.
- Ideas, thoughts, beliefs, and attitudes should be shared.
- Often results in a feeling of vulnerability.
- Open, honest, and candid discussion is a necessity.
(#11 Realistic Expectations)

Anticipation

- Process is dynamic.
- It evolves and changes.
- Persuasion, negotiation, and cooperation are common place.
- Resolutions may differ greatly from expectations.
(#12 Realistic Expectations)

Closure

- Deters discussion.
- Does not guarantee understanding or agreement.
- High-closure individuals may be impatient with the process.
- Sharing takes time.
- Closure does not always equal a solution.
(#3 Unrealistic Expectations)

Complaints

- Airing frustrations may be valid even if immediate alternatives are unknown.
- A demonstrable attitude of problem solving is required.
- Chronic complaints may deteriorate to offensive/defensive interaction.
(#6 Unrealistic Expectations)

The above highlights reflect concerns that normally appear as questions or session behaviors. Individual Facilitators, of course, may choose to highlight whichever items best suit their group needs and personal style.

Finally, there needs to be a balance between direction and restriction. After establishing the general process parameters, the Facilitator usually presents a brief session outline or agenda to provide this balance. The format should be broad and as flexible as possible. A rule of thumb is: No more than three to five main points, and perhaps one or two subpoints.

An agenda should serve only as the most general of guidelines. It is not meant to restrict or inhibit the discussion process itself. Unfortunately, many Facilitators routinely sacrifice discussion in order to cover all agenda items. This generates a false sense of closure, and may prematurely end the session before any real conclusions are reached. If decisions are made, they may be inaccurate or inadequate, and the cycle will almost certainly repeat itself at a later date. In either case, it would be preferable to decrease the number of agenda items and allow greater flexibility to pursue thinking patterns and underlying assumptions.

The agenda should provide an overall direction and reiterate the intended session goal. Any remaining questions the Participants have regarding the process should be answered at this time. This question/answer exchange will assist the Facilitator in assessing group readiness and acceptance of the process.

After

A final, integral part of preparation is to anticipate the debriefings and possible follow-ups. One type of debriefing occurs at the close of the session with Participants. Normally, it is called a review or summary. The purpose is to come "full circle" in the facilitation process, and provide psychological closure to the session itself. Progress is retraced, and the Participants' efforts are confirmed.

On completion of the session, a second type of debriefing occurs. Although it is imperative that this be held as soon afterward as possible, the Facilitator should determine the physical and psychological readiness of those involved. There are times when the session has been too physically or emotionally exhausting to make an immediate debriefing profitable. For maximum benefit, "as soon as possible" generally ranges from right after the session to thirty-six hours following.

Both the Facilitator and the Producer should be aware of this less observed, but equally important aspect of facilitation. The events, information exchanged, and decisions made during the session must be reviewed. The debriefing should include the Facilitator, the Producer and key associates. If a third party client is involved, they also should be present.

A third party client is an agent, consultant, or any other individual who has finalized the contract with the Provider (Facilitator). Although labeled differently, this relationship is actually quite common in facilitation, and has many advantages. One disadvantage, however, is that third party clients may want to conduct the debriefing themselves, without the Facilitator present. Meeting with the Producer and key associates, however, is the only way the Facilitator can assure that information has been accurately translated and disseminated. Direct interaction removes the impact of "translation error" and decreases the probability of miscommunication.

The debriefing should reflect a verbal tracking of the session's progress. It should include a review of the intended goals and the tangible results of Participant involvement. Deviations or unexpected developments of goals or issues can be examined and put into proper context. In addition, commitment and trust levels can be re-assessed.

Another reason for debriefing is to acknowledge previously unidentified goals and expectations. No matter how well Participants and Producers are prepared, some expectations simply do not surface until after the session. Of course, these may be unplanned (subconscious) or planned (hidden agenda) expectations. To overlook either of them is a common, but often professionally tragic flaw. The transient nature of their relationship with the group makes Facilitators particularly vulnerable to scapegoating. In addition, unresolved expectations can drastically affect the implementation of outcomes.

Effective debriefing can assist in reviewing goals, re-establishing responsibilities, and properly realigning expectations. During this meeting, the Facilitator has an added opportunity to emphasize what was learned through the process. Producers often have difficulty recognizing progress at each step even though it almost always occurs.

"Progress" actually takes a variety of forms and is, therefore, difficult for many people to discern. An experienced Facilitator can identify and interpret types of "progress" that otherwise would go unnoticed. A quick debriefing is no substitute for an in-depth analysis. It is, however, an opportunity for the Facilitator to orient Producers to their new roles as translators.

It is absolutely critical that Producers and their <u>key</u> associates enter the analysis-translator role with an open mindset. First, they must be willing to set aside their preconceptions of "progress" and "accomplishment." Second, they must accept their responsibility to actually search out <u>anything</u> that might be learned from a review of the session's interactions and behaviors. This much needed analysis can be simplified by a generic tool.

Figure 3.7 REFERENCE GUIDE FOR ANALYSIS

WHAT IS PROGRESS?

Progress is made through psychological and/or behavioral movement.

It should result in the ultimate betterment of those involved.

Progress may not be immediately recognizable.

Change and creativity are preceded by conflict.

Overall development occurs at both the individual and the group level.

Progress evolves through stages:

Exposure - Opportunity to consider information and alternatives.

Awareness - Acknowledgment of differing perspectives.

Internalization - Recognition and acceptance of selected viewpoints.

Action - Behavioral demonstration of incorporated attitudes.

EXAMPLES

Unexpected or alternative outcomes redirect the focus or pave the way for true problem identification.

Confrontation occurs and is resolved through discussion and negotiation.

Participants discover that they have focused on symptoms rather than problems.

Apprehensions, fears, or negative beliefs surface during the process.

Participant skills develop along a continuum: Novice - Proficient.

A previously silent individual shows vulnerability by voicing opinions and sharing ideas.

Sanctioned Participants realize they have been operating outside group norms, and alter their behaviors accordingly.

The Producer must realize the significance of the above analysis and what it explains about the group's ability to problem solve. The analysis should lead the Producer to reassess the session's original goals and objectives. Given the analysis, would the original goals be restated? What outcomes emerged in addition to or instead of the ones anticipated? How can maximum benefit be obtained from the process?

Further, debriefing allows the Facilitator to start what is actually another preparation phase. Whether or not the Facilitator continues to work with the group, there are encouragements and warnings about the group process that can be instilled. Just a few words of what to expect can deflect serious discouragement. Reference guides for both Producers and Participants can provide an understanding of the many variables involved in group development.

(HANDOUT)

Figure 3.8 PRODUCER GUIDE FOR GROUP DEVELOPMENT

Participants need management's validation and encouragement of the process.

Groups may "slip back" into their own comfortable, but less than effective, mode of operation without the aid of a Facilitator.

There is often Participant concern that their input will have little impact.

Group progress may not move as quickly or as smoothly without the Facilitator.

Although the group may have shown initial enthusiasm for the process and its outcomes, doubts may arise once the Facilitator is gone.

Groups may continue to have difficulty separating information dissemination items from discussion items.

Without a Facilitator, groups initially attempt to address the easiest, rather than the more difficult issues.

Difficult issues require more time for discussion and negotiation.

As the group matures, members may experience periods of frustration without a Facilitator to navigate through emotional or highly volatile issues.

Both developing and advanced groups should be audited periodically by an outsider who can monitor group functioning.

(HANDOUT)

Figure 3.9   PARTICIPANT GUIDE FOR GROUP DEVELOPMENT

Group progress may not move as quickly or as smoothly without the Facilitator.

Although the group may have shown initial enthusiasm for the process and its outcomes, doubts may arise once the Facilitator is gone.

Groups may continue to have difficulty separating information dissemination items from discussion items.

Initially, groups attempt to address the easiest, rather than the more difficult issues.

Difficult issues require more time for discusssion and negotiation.

As the group matures, members may experience periods of frustration without a Facilitator to navigate through emothional or highly volatile issues.

Both developing and advanced groups should be audited periodically by an outsider who can monitor group functioning.

These reactions and behaviors are normal, and do not necessarily mean the process has failed. It is at this point the Producer must be particularly careful to tangibly support the advancement of group problem-solving skills. If the Producer reinforces the process activities and initial commitment, many of these "blips" can be diffused or entirely avoided. A continuous nurturing of the group and the process itself is necessary for ongoing growth and development.

Finally, there are a variety of follow-ups available to the Producer and the Facilitator. Three of the more common options include summaries, oral reports, and written analyses.

Summaries are usually a written compilation of the group's input during the session. Typically, they are organized by topic, or by the group's indicated priority ranking. These are almost always included as a service by the Facilitator.

Oral reports are normally in addition to, rather than in place of, a written summary. They provide the Producer with a quick and informal assessment of the group's functioning.

Written analyses are more in-depth and formalized. They provide a complete analysis of the content discussed against the context of group behavior. In most cases, it is a separately negotiated service from the Facilitator.

Following is an overview of process guidelines.

Figure 3.10 PROCESS GUIDELINE SUMMARY		
Before	**During**	**After**

Reference Guide on Facilitation	Rights of Respect	Debriefing
		   Session Summary
		   Session Analysis

Producer Orientation	Highlights	Reference Guide for Analysis
Participant Orientation	Written Agenda/ Outline	Producer Guide for Group Development

Options
   Interviews
   Focus Instrument
		Participant Guide for Group Development

		Follow-ups
		   Summaries
		   Oral Reports
		   Written Analyses

The facilitation process challenges the abilities, experience, and expertise of the group to meet its maximum potential. It allows for guiding a discussion without narrowing its scope or setting time limits. Facilitators should work within this productive middle ground that neither completely abandons, nor rigidly adheres to guidelines.

A solid orientation reduces barriers and lessens the number of unknowns. This preparation promotes the possibility for understanding and acceptance (not necessarily agreement) of the process. These steps, in turn, can create the most receptive forum for the introduction and development of ideas.

PSYCHOLOGICAL

GROUP BACKGROUND

No one can guarantee a "perfectly" conducive environment. There are certain aspects, however, that so strongly impact the process, they demand the Facilitator's attention. Two of the most vital are the group members' backgrounds, and their perceptions of the process and the Facilitator.

Individual Experiences

A seemingly obvious statement is that groups are comprised of individuals. Despite this observation, many Facilitators and Producers tend to overlook or dismiss its implications. Each member brings to the group process their own sets of beliefs, assumptions, experiences, biases, expectations, memories, and skills.

Trying to fully appreciate the myriad of impressions and motivations from just <u>one</u> individual is difficult at best. Even the most astute Facilitator is overwhelmed. Further, it becomes more difficult and is all the more intricate as group membership increases. To make sense of these perceptions, we rely on language and a fundamental understanding of nonverbal communication.

Language, however exacting, is often grossly inadequate to convey thoughts and emotions alike. The Facilitator has the prime responsibility for the translation of these concepts. An easy route to avoid confusion is to see only commonalties. In other words, rather than trying to discern differences, some may choose to concentrate on similarities.

Recognizing similarities among group members is a useful tool. Perceiving and utilizing only these, however, is counterproductive. People <u>are</u> different. They feel, perceive, and think differently, and it is these differences that provide group negotiation with its life-blood.

Collective History

Facilitators and Producers must also understand that groups, like individuals, acquire, interpret, and pass on their collective memory to new members and outsiders. The group itself is not just a sum of its members. Synergy allows it to take on a life of its own.

A group that has not previously met (zero history), will quickly begin to devise norms, develop patterns of communication, and track its own progress. Further, if the group has been meeting (non-zero history), it is important for the Facilitator to assess its viability as an effective group. Working with either zero or non-zero history groups has both advantages and disadvantages.

Zero History Advantages

- No historical barriers specific to the group.

- Enthusiasm for new experience.

- May be an opportunity to select individual members with specific skills/expertise.

- Fewer sanctions against individual process mistakes.

- May be more open to suggestions concerning group functioning.

Zero History Disadvantages

- No proven track record.

- Individual biases have not yet been mitigated by group involvement.

- May be apprehensive or fearful of the group process.

- High number of unknowns make group functioning uncomfortable.

- Unwilling members have not yet been exposed to peer pressure.

Non-Zero History Advantages

- Opportunity for members to have worked with one another.

- May have had the experience of productive problem solving.

- May be seasoned in negotiating and reaching consensus.

- Individuals may already share in the functions of group leadership.

- Positive peer pressure may already be present.

Non-Zero History Disadvantages

- Individuals may have experienced disillusionment with the group.

- Group may have a history of no consensus.

- May have developed a pattern of conflict avoidance.

- Counterproductive coalitions may be present.

- Group may suffer from tunnel vision.

It should be noted that productive groups of either type (zero/non-zero) may show none of the above disadvantages. Conversely, nonproductive groups of either type may show none of the above advantages.

GROUP PERCEPTION

In addition to its members, the group itself holds perceptions concerning both the process and the Facilitator. Perceptions, like biases, may be positive or negative. Positive perceptions are most likely to spawn cooperative attitudes. For the most part, these are easily recognized by the Facilitator. Negative perceptions, on the other hand, may require closer inspection.

An extreme reaction is obvious, but many negative attitudes fall along a continuum of intensity. In addition, it is a western cultural norm to withhold or mask negative responses. This makes the Facilitator's job of discernment all the more difficult, and the consequences all the more dangerous.

The Facilitator's strongest ally is a receptive and open frame of mind. Jumping to an immediate conclusion that a single action is positive or negative will eliminate or bias any other possible interpretations. Entertaining alternative motivations for Participant behavior helps balance and ground a Facilitator in reality. It can prevent the psychological paralysis caused either by overconfidence or rejection.

Openness can prevent paralysis resulting from excessively positive or negative biases. Overconfidence (positive bias) brings on a feeling of complacency that dulls the Facilitator's effectiveness. Rejection (negative bias) tends to lessen the Facilitator's willingness to take risks. Either extreme, or any unproductive point in between can impair the Facilitator's ability to function.

MULTIPLE ROLES

Individuals are often required to perform more than one role. This is especially true of Producers who may also be acting as Participants, and Participants who may be asked to facilitate.

Producer/Participant

Given proper preparation, Producers should have a basic awareness of the Participant's role and responsibilities. A larger problem with this multiple role depends on other Participants' perceptions. If for no other reason than position or status, Producers need to be sensitive to the reactions of all group members.

Participants often feel inhibited or even threatened by a Producer's presence. Discussion may be severely limited or too veiled in political rhetoric to be of any direct value. Awareness of these potential reactions can help both the Producer and the Facilitator anticipate any potential impact on group outcomes.

This circumstance is a vivid example of shared responsibility. When the above or similar responses are noticed, the Facilitator, the Producer, and the other Participants have the responsibility of creating a more comfortable environment, and drawing out one another's views. Further, each group member has a personal responsibility to make every effort to overcome the tendency to withhold or deliberately alter the true message they wish to convey.

Participant/Facilitator

The Participant who is asked to facilitate, faces unique challenges. Fundamentally, there is the issue of skills. Facilitator skills are complex, integrated abilities. Although training is a necessary component, it simply cannot cover all possibilities.

The range of necessary skills should not discourage individuals from seeking training. Rather, it should place the acquisition and application of training in perspective. No matter how extensive, tennis lessons are not equivalent to playing the professional circuit. Professional Facilitators not only possess more training, but have the added advantage of constant practice.

In addition to their skills, Participants turned Facilitators are placed in a tenuous position. They may be unfamiliar or uncomfortable working with those of higher status. They may see facilitation as a distraction from their "real" job and rush or cut short the process. Further, in this new position, they may be pressured by others to favor or endorse a particular stance.

Possessing and maintaining an objective position on all issues may be difficult for the Participant/Facilitator. If they have expressed a strong position prior to the session, objectivity is in even greater jeopardy. The results of this subjective involvement can range from feelings of intimidation, to loss of leadership, to a complete manipulation of the session's development.

Any or all of the above issues can contribute to a group's passive or active rejection of the Participant/Facilitator. Group members may question the individual's skill, resulting in mistrust and a vague apprehension of process validity. As peers, they may harbor suspicions concerning the Participant/Facilitator's motives and allegiances.

This last point is particularly true when interests close to the Facilitator are examined. It is unreasonable to expect anyone to remain dispassionate and objective while listening to a discussion of their "own" issues. Further, Participants, already cautious of Facilitator bias, are likely to assume the worst. As a result, both the Facilitator and the process may be discredited.

Once any individual's role or position in the organization has been established, it is difficult to gain acceptance for a role change, be it temporary or permanent. It takes time, patience, the building of new trust bridges, and a high degree of flexibility by the Participant/Facilitator to effect this change. Common sense precautions concerning objectivity and a demonstration of solid Facilitator skills can help cement this new group relationship.

PHYSICAL

The physical environment for facilitation cannot be underestimated. Humans are not just composites of thoughts and emotions. They are visceral beings, sensitive and responsive to the elements surrounding them.

Since facilitation is a dynamic process, it is not likely that every contingency will be anticipated. There are, however, suggestions for the most frequently encountered decision areas: Geographic Location; Room; Lighting; Air; Food and Beverages; and Interruptions.

GEOGRAPHIC LOCATION

Choosing a site for sessions is a task that should be done with considerable care and attention to detail. Since it will be the backdrop for all activities, it must meet group needs while supporting overall goals.

If quiet and solitude are important, a suburban or country location would be more appropriate than an urban site. This type of site would curb many distractions. On the other hand, if easy in/out access on a long term basis is critical, then a centrally located urban location would be more suitable to continuous participation. No matter which of these alternatives is chosen, relatively easy and safe accessibility is important.

A second point in choice of location is the consideration of on-site versus off-site. There are pros and cons, of course, with either decision. As a rule, off-site is preferable, primarily because a clearer distinction can be made between current job responsibilities and session commitment. Consequently, there is less guilt or confusion regarding priorities. On-site locations are, however, acceptable as long as uninterrupted privacy can be maintained. Unless this assurance is in place, sessions, as well as their outcomes, can be severely affected.

ROOM

Sometimes Facilitators have little or no choice concerning available rooms. Other times, they may be given "free reign" in choosing both location and setting. Regardless of freedom, there are a few guidelines that, if at all possible, should be followed.

Size

This should be determined by its appropriateness for the group. There needs to be enough space to move and maneuver freely during small group activities (although this may vary with cultural backgrounds). On the other hand, rooms too large are equally, and ironically, constricting. Too much space often produces feelings of tension and anxiety. Facilitators should attempt to remove or add walls and/or screen partitions.

Setting

Again, this should be appropriate for the group and the task at hand. An arrangement should be chosen that allows maximum potential for interaction. There are a variety of configurations available to the Facilitator.

Traditional Setting - Typically, this includes groupings such as U-shaped, Half-circle, Conference style and Circular.

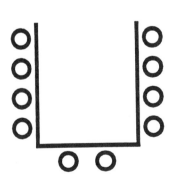

U-shaped arrangements provide an opportunity for face-to-face interaction among the Participants, while allowing the Facilitator optional movement in and out of direct group territory. A common difficulty with this seating is that there may be too much distance across the "U." This results in a feeling of separation or division, and can actually encourage the formation of undesirable coalitions.

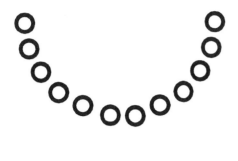

Half-circles are used with or without tables. They offer relatively good face-to-face interaction, although the Facilitator should be aware that <u>any</u> seating arrangement without "marker furniture (tables, dividers, counters)" is subject to "shape shifting." In other words, half-circles may become full circles, rectangles, triangles, or any other random shape. These shifts should be closely monitored for Participant alienation and interaction intensity.

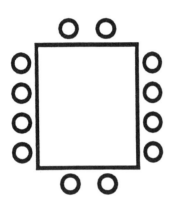

Conference style is one of the most frequently used arrangements. Although conducive to the face-to-face interaction patterns of the "U," it normally maintains closer proximity among Participants. One characteristic of this style that some Facilitators dislike is that it restricts their own physical movements in and out of direct interaction lines.

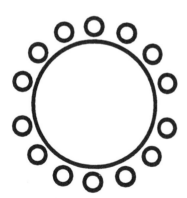

Circular table seating is a variation of the Conference style. Even though there are many similarities to the square or rectangle conference arrangement, this style equalizes most power positions. In general, the smaller the circle, the more informal and intimate the setting. The larger the circle, the more formal and rigid the setting.

Larger-Scale Seating - These arrangements are varied. Three of the most common layouts include:

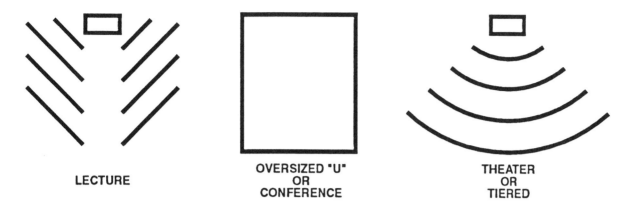

LECTURE   OVERSIZED "U"   THEATER
                     OR   OR
                 CONFERENCE   TIERED

Whatever their form, the styles have one dominant characteristic. For facilitative purposes, they are all difficult.

Ideally, the Facilitator is allowed to reduce the number of Participants per session, and find alternate seating arragements. Like all circumstances, however, there are exceptions. On occasion, it may become necessary to accommodate a larger number of Participants than was originally anticipated. In any case, the Facilitator's responsibility is to minimize physical distance among individuals and maximize interaction.

Informal Seating - There are opportunities to experiment with alternative seating arrangements (couches, overstuffed chairs, and so on).

Use or non-use of these arrangements is primarily a matter of personal choice by the Facilitator. Alternating this style with more formal settings can increase intimacy and cooperation. It should be noted, however, that such furnishings are relaxing for Participants and may result in decreased energy levels.

Many of the above difficulties can be controlled by using "break-out" periods during the session. Large groups can be subdivided into groups of five to nine, and even smaller groups can be separated into twos (dyads) or threes.

Break-outs may be accommodated by rearranging furniture in the session room. If this does not provide enough space and privacy for small group interaction, then separate rooms or lounges should be made available for these discussion periods. Physically, break-outs are used both to decrease frustration and anxiety, and to energize Participants.

In summary, the choice of seating arrangements is an important component of the comfortability and potential productivity of group Participants. Facilitators should be prepared to request an appropriate setting. They should be equally prepared, however, to adjust to whatever conditions they encounter. As always, the central criterion should be maximum member participation.

Color

Room color impacts the well being of Participants. It has a direct bearing on their attitudes and comfort levels. Bright, hot colors such as yellow, orange, and red can precipitate feelings of high anxiety and/or tension. Comfort levels drop, spontaneity disappears, and over time, discussion can become choppy and nonproductive.

Conversely, colors such as green and blue promote a calm, peaceful, and tranquil setting. As a result, they provide a more neutral background for discussion and problem solving. Generally, this color scheme has little or no distracting effect on Participant comfort levels.

A common mistake is choosing a room with plain, white walls thinking that this is a neutral color. In fact, white, empty walls are stark and quite intimidating to many people. They carry an institutional influence and tend to stilt or impede group growth and development.

A rule of thumb is to choose a room where color forms a subtle background, rather than one in which color makes a bold statement. This will decrease, at least in some measure, potentially disruptive environmental variables.

LIGHTING

Essentially, there are two types of lighting: Natural and artificial. Each of them in their own way can affect participation.

Natural lighting in a room generally comes from windows, doors, or skylights. The size, shape, position, and geographic direction of these openings can alter room conditions through the course of a session. There may be no constant amount or intensity of light. This results in unpredictable fluctuations in light depending on the time of day and existing weather conditions.

To equalize this condition, artificial light is supplemented as needed. Caution should be exercised, however, since a correlation often exists between intensity of light and anxiety levels. Usually, the greater the intensity, the higher the anxiety. An optimum setting, of course, should be determined by what the Facilitator ultimately wants to accomplish.

By itself, artificial lighting is easier to regulate and control. It allows one to adjust for dark walls, high ceilings, and shadows. At the same time, however, tension, tiredness or even feelings of claustrophobia can result from limited or no natural lighting. Some people (including Facilitators) are simply uncomfortable with rooms containing no windows and/or only artificial light sources.

Both the Facilitator and the Producer need to share in a basic understanding of the Participants' preferences and needs. Remember, light can be soothing or intimidating, encouraging or hindering. The objective is to make it a practical, yet subtle part of the overall environment.

AIR

The "invisible" environment can have a dramatic influence on Participant comfortability. Surrounding temperature and air quality can enhance or exhaust energy, tolerance, and concentration levels.

Temperature

During their careers, professional Facilitators typically experience a full range of temperature exposure. Air conditioning can easily chill rooms to the 50's, while central heating can overwhelm Participants with 90+ degrees.

To determine prime comfort, there are obvious signals to watch for in those present (coats on or off; standing or pacing; falling asleep; use of fans, etc.). The not so obvious (awareness; understanding of basic physical differences), however, are perhaps the most important, since they may also act as preventative measures.

First and foremost, individuals vary as much in physical preferences as they do in any other area. What works well for one, may not be tolerable for another. Second, while determining a proper compromise, keep in mind that the Facilitator may be perceptually biased. Moving from group to group, speaking, and recording comments may result in feeling "too warm" when the temperature is quite cold.

The risk run by ignoring climatic conditions is lowered involvement, increased (and often unnecessary) disagreements, a push for premature closure, and diminished cooperation. When in doubt, a check can always be made by periodically asking the Participants. Ultimately, if room temperature is too extreme and unable to be controlled, session outcomes might well benefit from a change of location.

Quality

In addition to temperature, a fresh, odor-free environment contributes to a neutral background. One of the most frequently encountered questions concerning neutrality is the issue of tobacco smoke. Some Participants may not be bothered by smoke, some may be irritated or have allergic reactions. Psychologically, it may even create barriers among Participants -- smokers don't wish to sit with non-smokers, non-smokers don't wish to share the room with smokers.

74

Many organizations have established a standard "no smoking" policy. Some, however, have not, and the meeting itself may be held at off-site, non-regulated locations. In these optional environments, it is the Facilitator's decision.

Pros and cons aside, the safest approach is to adhere to a "no smoking" policy during the session, with relatively close smoking areas for breaks. As with color and lighting, temperature and particularly air quality are vital to producing optimal participative conditions.

FOOD AND BEVERAGES

Food

Snack food of one kind or another is almost always provided during sessions. The types and times of its availability may dramatically affect group performance. These effects manifest themselves both chemically and mechanically.

Food containing a high processed sugar content (sweet rolls, candy, etc.) give immediate energy boosts that fade quickly. This can provoke erratic spurts of energy which may detract from or make more difficult a focused discussion. Conversely, foods with natural sugar or those with protein (fruit, cheese, etc.) will generate longer lasting energy levels. As a result, this latter group enables the Facilitator to help stabilize Participants' stamina. Choices should also address specific dietary needs and cultural considerations.

When snacks are to be included, they should be available throughout the session. Foods served should be easy to handle. Items that require distractive preparation before consumption diminish concentration. Shells, peelings, and wrappers are somewhat messy and noisy. If they are present, ample containers should be provided for their quick disposal. This eliminates set-up distraction and allows Participants the freedom to choose their own time to satisfy a craving.

Oftentimes, meals are served in conjunction with full-day sessions. Lunches are most commonly targeted for this type of catering, and, if possible, should be set up outside the working session room. It is, of course, strictly Facilitator preference whether "assignments" (group discussions or projects) continue during this time. Disadvantages may be reflected in sporadic conversation and disjointed groups, while advantages include extra time and continuity of discussion.

Beverages

The standard array of beverages includes coffee, tea, and/or juice in the morning, and carbonated (non-alcoholic) drinks in the afternoon. Perhaps the largest difficulty with this arrangement is that it is actually quite restrictive in choice. Many people drink coffee or tea during the afternoon, and there are those who prefer carbonated beverages in the morning.

Within cultural contexts, there should be as much variety as possible. At a minimum, water, coffee, teas, chocolate, carbonated drinks, and juices should be available for the duration of the session. Further, caffeinated, decaffeinated, and dietetic options should always be part of these choices.

Alcohol during evening sessions is sometimes an issue. Ideally, a "no-alcohol" policy should be followed. This is particularly true if alcohol is available during the social hour or meal preceding the session.

In general, the Producer has the responsibility for providing food and beverages. The Facilitator, however, should offer input and justification as necessary. Failure to provide satisfying and dietetically diverse offerings can cause Participant agitation and loss of concentration. As a result, availability and choice of these items can directly impact session productivity.

INTERRUPTIONS

There are a myriad of interruptions that can occur during a session. Those listed below, however, are among the most common. Each one of these is distracting and can result in a serious break in concentration.

It is interesting to note that Producers are oftentimes the cause of interruptions. It is not only the Participant, then, who is responsible for breaks in process. Producers or their messengers move in and out of groups, keep Participants from arriving on time, or call them out of sessions. In addition, since Producers hold a higher status than Participants, their behavior is rarely questioned. As a result, they do not receive or feel the pressure of sanctions that would be levied on other Participants.

Participants absent during instructions or discussions miss vital segments of the process and ask inappropriate questions. Further, they may request updates while the rest of the group is trying to move forward, thus annoying or irritating other members.

Specific types of interruptions pose particular difficulties for Facilitators. A more detailed look at each one can provide insights for prevention and correction.

Late Arrivals/Early Departures - Late arrivals miss orientation information and applicable instructions. Their presence may require adjustments in seating arrangements or group divisions. In some instances, they may even be ignored or shunned by other group members. Early departures, as well as late arrivals, are frequently seen as disrespectful behaviors.

Jack-in-the-Box Syndrome - The individual is constantly up and down during the session. This disconnection/reconnection is probably one of the most disconcerting sets of behavior for other group members. The pattern originates from telephone calls, messages, beepers, or pagers. With some individuals, it may just occur spontaneously, for no apparent outside reason. It is not surprising that individuals with this syndrome are often seen as "lesser" group members, or even renegades by their peers.

Beepers - Audio versions are more distracting than motion (vibrating) types. Despite the differences in initial contact, however, the results are often the same -- too many interruptions which occur too often, are too costly to individual satisfaction and group productivity.

Messages - As a general policy, messages should be posted on a common access board outside of the session room, unless absolutely urgent.

Telephones - If possible, telephones should not be present in the session room unless under direct Facilitator supervision. There are occasions when group members <u>must</u> be contacted, and <u>must</u> return the call. Normally, however, this exchange of information can wait until a break point. Break times, of course, should provide ample opportunity for telephone calling. A simple calculation of break length should consider the number of Participants versus the number of telephones available.

Physical interruptions are distracting and directly impact session goals. At worst, the individuals involved are seen as disrespectful, uninterested, and may even be ostracized by their peers. At best, they may be tolerated, but their fluctuation in involvement usually hinders full participation in discussions and decision making. It is no wonder that the less experienced Facilitator becomes flustered and may lose group focus and productive momentum.

An equally important key to minimizing interruptions is effective prioritization. There <u>are</u> emergencies that require immediate attention. Most often, however, messages identified as "urgent" are actually concerns or points of information that, while important, can be addressed during breaks, meals, or after sessions.

These issues illustrate the need for a solid process orientation which includes ground rules to curb the number and type of interruptions. Consideration for the group as a whole must always be the central focus.

CHAPTER SUMMARY

The stronger the working link between the Producer and the Facilitator, the stronger and more beneficial will be the process. Desire, commitment, and trust are the key elements necessary for session preparation and monitoring. It is in this arena that the Producer has an equal, if not greater power than the Facilitator to directly impact session success or failure.

First, there must be a solid commitment by the Producer to provide the Facilitator with all pertinent information regarding the organization and group members. Second, both the Producer and the Facilitator have dual responsibility to prepare the group for participation and ensure that the physical environment is suitable for their work.

Finally, the "environment" should meet psychological as well as physical needs. Unexpected events are, of course, always a possibility, but extensive preparation can minimize any impact. An ongoing analysis and a constant clarification of goals can substantially raise the odds for a productive session. This context, then, becomes the backdrop against which the process and the content of facilitation occurs.

IV. THE ENERGY
(Abilities)

Preparation, procedures, and guidelines are indispensable in facilitation. Despite all of this pre-planning, it is ultimately the Facilitator's personal abilities that become the focal point of a successful process.

The skills required for effective facilitation can be broken into three distinct and progressively difficult levels:

Informative - Structure, Direction, Objectives, Feedback, Focus, Explanation.

Interpretive - Listening, Flexibility, Separation, Openness, Process, Translate.

Intuitive - Create, Instinct, Timing, Empathy, Synthesize, Integrate.

The Informative level skills are largely one-directional. That is, they are directed either from the Facilitator to the Participants, or in the case of feedback, from the Participants to the Facilitator. In addition, the skills in this grouping are not necessarily dependent on one another.

The Interpretive and Intuitive level skills, however, are more two-directional. There is a more intense, simultaneous exchange of energy and involvement between the Facilitator and the Participants. In addition, the skills in these groups are more interdependent. As such, it is necessary for the Facilitator to continuously blend and balance their application.

The skills within these levels are specific, though not inclusive. For each listed, there are minimal requirements for competency and examples of how their presence or absence impacts group productivity.

SKILLS

Informative

Structure - Develop agendas/establish climate.

Requirements

* Possess sense of organization.
* Construct logical flow.
* Coordinate people and activities.
* Recognize the need for preparation and design appropriate tools.
* Balance group needs with environmental limitations.

Impact

When Present . . .
* Fewer misunderstandings concerning progress results in less time to reach the productivity stage.
* Fewer unknowns resulting in higher confidence and trust levels among Participants and Producers.
* Participants and Producers are more apt to accept and act on their individually assigned responsibilities.
* When "blips" do occur, Participants are more likely to make corrections themselves.

When Absent . . .
* Produces feelings of anxiety.
* Individuals do not understand or even recognize their roles and responsibilities.
* Participants do not perceive a sense of flow and continuity.
* Environmental "blips" become major focal points rather than minor adjustments.

Informative

Direction - Move toward a goal.

Requirements

* Construct logical flow.
* Adjust group's energy and focus.
* Direct efforts of individual members toward a common group goal.
* Reactivate stalled discussions.
* Exercise patience with the process as a whole.

Impact

When Present . . .
* Contributes to the Participants' perceptions of progress.
* Participants are more likely to respond to prodding from an outside Facilitator.
* Easier to track goal alignments among individual members.

When Absent . . .
* When the Facilitator does not demonstrate patience, there is no role model for Participants to follow.
* Results in an insidious erosion of Participant confidence in the process.
* Produces choppy, uneven movement during discussions.
* Loss of group energy and momentum.

Informative

Objectives - To identify the main steps needed to reach the overall goal.

Requirements

* Construct a logical flow.
* Develop a mental sequence of steps needed in the process.
* Moves steps from broad to progressively more specific concepts.
* Balance push for closure with need for further discussion.
* Sift and sort information for similarities and connections.

Impact

When Present . . .
* Participants are able to more clearly see movement toward an overall goal.
* As objectives are devised, Participants are able to sense incremental accomplishments.
* Develop Participant skills to identify components within goals.
* Deviations from goals are more easily recognized.

When Absent . . .
* Participants flounder in attempts to break down the overall goal into manageable steps.
* Results in perceptions of confusion and duplication among objectives.
* Participants who doubt the Facilitator's mental "road map" will experience greater uncertainty and heightened anxiety.

Informative

Feedback -To respond verbally and nonverbally to Participant input.

Requirements

* Restate Participant input as accurately as possible.
* Distinguish between precise feedback and liberal interpretation.
* Recognize and identify completed thoughts in Participant commentary.
* Discern and acknowledge nonverbal Participant input.

Impact

When Present . . .

* By receiving Facilitator feedback, Participants' input is acknowledged.
* Allows Participants an opportunity to hear informal summaries.
* Allows Participants to check and then clarify their message.
* Encourages more reticent group members to participate.

When Absent . . .

* Participants are uncertain as to whether or not the message was received.
* Participants lack the opportunity to check their own input.
* Produces anxiety, since there is no indication of acceptance or rejection.

Informative

Focus - To maintain direction and purpose.

Requirements

* Maintain a logical flow throughout discussions.
* Redirect random discussions.
* Identify and summarize discussion benchmarks.
* Provide central energy and concentration behind group momentum.
* Balance push for closure with need for further discussion.

Impact

When Present . . .
* Facilitator acts as a resource to provide historical continuity to discussions.
* Serves as a role model for Participants to check their own focus.
* Develops patience in Participants for working through periods of slow discussion or misunderstanding.
* Allows Participants to evaluate group progress with a Facilitator to group progress without a Facilitator.

When Absent . . .
* Dominant group member may assume leadership of the group.
* Produces inconsistent energy flow.
* Without focus, individual contributions may be overlooked or minimized.
* Results in Participant loss of direction and premature closure.

Informative

Explanation - To instruct in or clarify definitions and concepts.

Requirements

* Develop an understanding as best possible of the organization's agreed-on goals.
* Possess a sense of organization.
* Communicate instructions in a simple and straightforward manner.
* Exercise patience to re-explain or expand instructions and definitions.
* Utilize a full range of knowledge concerning groups and their interaction patterns.

Impact

When Present . . .
* Allows members who otherwise might be overwhelmed by a large goal to approach it through step-by-step instructions.
* Completion of instructions provides natural "pauses" during the session to review group progress.
* Encourages group members to clarify their own thoughts and concepts.
* Explanations and instructions raise Participant comfort levels, and help align expectations.

When Absent . . .
* Participants may not understand the wording used by the Facilitator to disseminate instructions.
* Misunderstood instructions can waste group energy.
* Unclear explanations may result in unnecessary resistance and opposition by group members.
* Impatient Facilitators result in group members' reluctance to ask for clarification.

SKILLS

Interpretive

Listening - Comprehend both the denotative and connotative parts of a
     message.

Requirements

> * Sensitivity to nonverbal signals.
> * Exercise patience and the use of silence with Participants.
> * Merge both verbal and nonverbal components into a cohesive
>   message.
> * Project an open-minded and non-judgmental attitude while listening.

Impact

When Present . . .
> * The process of listening and providing feedback demonstrates
>   Facilitator involvement.
> * Provides the basis for understanding and negotiated compromise.
> * Encourages more vulnerable communication among Participants.

When Absent . . .
> * Inhibits open and candid discussion.
> * Seasoned Participants feel resentment or anger.
> * Novice Participants are unwilling or hesitant to offer or interject
>   commentary.

Interpretive

Flexibility - To accept unknowns as assets in goal attainment.

Requirements

* Adjust to added insights concerning an organization, group, or individual.
* Compare and contrast contradictions between previously collected historical information and newly observed input.
* Accept divergent subject ideas while maintaining focus on the existing topics.
* Allow Participants the opportunity to express a wide range of emotions.

Impact

When Present . . .
* Maintain individual momentum and group process flow.
* A Facilitator's candid consideration of contradictions and opinions develops trust and demonstrates a sincere interest in the group.
* The Facilitator uses unknowns to assist Participants in exploring unconventional options to problems.

When Absent . . .
* Ignoring or denying the introduction of additional data may anger or alienate Participants.
* Participants are discouraged from offering thoughts or insights not directly relevant to the immediate discussion.
* Feeds the stereotypic notions that "disciplined thinking needs to be rigid" and "everyone thinks the way I do."

Interpretive

Separation - To distinguish among issues and provide a logical framework.

Requirements

* Discern factual from emotional components of the subject at hand.
* Identify and set aside peripheral issues for distinct consideration.
* Develop a chronological, topical, or cause/effect outline for analysis.
* Recognize and address the potential impact of any psychological ties among issues.

Impact

When Present . . .
* Is used as a tool to realign and maintain a focused discussion.
* Division of issues discourages generalizations and mitigates stereotyping.
* Thorough and systematic analysis increases the likelihood of uncovering the "root" cause.

When Absent . . .
* Incidents and issues overlap and become conceptually entangled.
* Discussions can become emotionally charged.
* Allows Participants the opportunity to raise "old" or "dead" issues which may adversely affect outcomes.

Interpretive

Openness - To acknowledge, understand, and manage emotions.

Requirements

* A willingness to connect with Participants' range of emotional states.
* Withhold judgment, while validating emotional and psychological responses of Participants.
* High degree of sensitivity in recognizing and reading nonverbal signals.
* Generate an invisible aura of receptivity toward Participants.
* Use body language to show visible confirmation of Participants' input.

Impact

When Present . . .
* Support Participants during times of emotional vulnerability and psychological stress.
* Identify and distinguish early signs of emotional conflict.
* Provide an environment that encourages reticent group members to actively participate in the process.

When Absent . . .
* Stifle participation by attitude, tone of voice, or negative language.
* Crucial nonverbal signals may be overlooked or not given serious consideration.
* Facilitator bias can narrow group discussion and/or limit idea exchange.

Interpretive

Process - To "read" and maintain the flow of interaction.

Requirements

* Monitor individual Participants to assess their active/passive involvement in group discussion.
* Conceptually view the group's interactions as fitting together into a cohesive whole.
* Review or offer a summation of past points to encourage expanded discussion.
* Comfortability with techniques that may expand or contract discussion as needed.
* Offer Participants periodic "readings" of trends/direction of discussion.

Impact

When Present . . .
* The Facilitator's role as historical/process monitor frees Participants to concentrate more on discussion and less on fine points and procedural requirements.
* Facilitator summaries also act as guideposts that can be used to measure progress.
* Facilitators place themselves as linking pins between Participants' input in order to build discussion points.
* Facilitators can identify and adjust for verbal and nonverbal fluctuations in individual contributions.

When Absent . . .
* Participants can become mired in detail and lose sight of the overall goal.
* Discussion points may remain underdeveloped or even dropped.
* Facilitators may use inappropriate discussion techniques which divert or hinder interaction.
* Premature or unnecessary termination of the group may occur.

Interpretive

Translate - To provide common meanings for definitions and concepts.

Requirements

* Use feedback to give Participants the opportunity to clarify and refine their input for more productive use by the group.
* Distinguish concepts from among a series of descriptive words.
* Continuously alter mental frameworks while listening to Participants.
* Separate denotative (dictionary definition) from connotative (psychological implications) meanings when necessary.
* Break down or explain unfamiliar concepts and/or terms to be used by the group.

Impact

When Present . . .
* Facilitator monitors Participant word usage and interjects with clarifications or definitions.
* Facilitator helps to prevent or diffuse emotionally volatile misunderstandings.
* Creates opportunities to provide extended examples.
* Through demonstration, the Facilitator encourages Participants to consider information from many perspectives.

When Absent . . .
* An absence of clear terms may result in discussion lag.
* Participants alone may not be able to "see" or "pull" useful concepts from the general flow of discussion.
* Participants may use unfamiliar jargon or other language which can result in confusion or rejection.
* Without a translator, individual Participants may feel misunderstood and, in extreme cases, alienated from the group process.

SKILLS

Intuitive

Create - To expand the agenda so as to encourage the development of
alternative views and sustain an open climate.

Requirements

* Restate Participant comments to stimulate broader discussion and
  analysis.
* Provide additional or extended examples which generate
  opportunities for new perspectives.
* Cultivate the group's capacity to develop alternative interpretations.
* Monitor and divert tendencies toward premature judgment.

Impact

When Present . . .
* Supports individual and group explorations of perceptions and ideas.
* Develops individual and group skills in alternative or non-traditional
  thinking.
* Compose and convey mental pictures for the Participants to assist
  them in understanding and nurturing concepts.
* Challenges Participants by examining previously discounted or
  contradictory perspectives.

When Absent . . .
* Without the ability to probe or expand, discussion may not be
  thoroughly developed.
* Personal bias can severely inhibit or entirely prevent idea exchange.
* Group members can become so tied to an agenda that difficult
  discussions are avoided.
* Participants may have a limited view of alternatives available to them
  on any given issue.

Intuitive

Instinct - To discuss meanings and utilize unknowns by spontaneously combining observation with experience.

Requirements

* Possess a low level apprehension for the uncertain or the unknown.
* Utilize both direct and indirect application of experiential knowledge.
* Superimpose current conditions over prior group history to determine ways to move the discussion forward.
* Deduce through observation and insight the similarities and differences of Participant thinking and language patterns.

Impact

When Present . . .
* Unknowns are presented and phrased in a tolerable fashion.
* Continuously combining and recombining concepts acts as a catalyst for Participant insight.
* The Facilitator's acceptance and willingness to work with unknowns instills greater confidence among group members to actively seek out new ideas.
* The Facilitator's use of instinct heightens Participants' awareness of their own and others' signals.

When Absent . . .
* Nuances and seemingly unimportant side comments go unnoticed or unchallenged.
* Uncertain about their own ability to discern, Participants favor greater formalization and rigidity of discussion.
* Participants may become so engrossed in discussion that multiple messages escape them.
* Without the practiced applications of instinct, hidden agendas may flourish and perpetuate.

Intuitive

Timing - To select the precise sequence and rate at which concepts are
processed for maximum effect.

Requirements

* Monitor the pulse of the environment in order to know when to make
changes or additions in the proceedings.
* Provide appropriate guidelines for regulating conversation.
* Stimulate the process at appropriate intervals through the interjection
of concepts and feelings.
* Decipher Participants' words and actions to determine when the
discussion has "played out."
* Anticipate the direction and overall meaning of individual comments.

Impact

When Present . . .
* Participants experience a greater sense of forward momentum.
* Alerts the group when discussion deviates too far.
* Discussion is interrupted to allow immediate input by reserved
members.
* Impacts the discussion through questions or comments in order to
provoke further development.

When Absent . . .
* Ideas can become tangled or lost in extended side conversations.
* Dominant members are more likely to monopolize the discussion.
* Group interest wanes when discussion control is abused or ignored.
* Inappropriately placed changes may damage the group's sense of
unity.

Intuitive

Empathy - To identify so completely with the Participant(s) that one shares as well as understands their experiences.

Requirements

* Superimpose any Participant's perspective over the Facilitator's own perceptions.
* Willingness to expand one's framework for interpreting situations, actions, and the surrounding environment.
* Seek and generate alternatives from using a Participant's point of view.
* Sense and develop a greater depth of meaning from both verbal and nonverbal messages.

Impact

When Present . . .
* Participants feel freer to express themselves without fear of rejection.
* Facilitator's empathy provides a concrete example for Participants to follow.
* Builds a bond of trust and shared meanings between the Facilitator and group members.
* Members are confident that every conscientious effort will be made to fully understand their views.

When Absent . . .
* Participants may feel misunderstood or even isolated from the group.
* A lack of mutual understanding among Participants diminishes contributions to the process.
* Discussion itself maintains narrow parameters and limited scope.
* Emotional components of issues may be overlooked or deliberately ignored.

Synthesize - To blend both similar and diverse ideas into understandable
concepts.

Requirements

> * Extract and mix basic components of ideas presented.
> * Discern the common elements among differing or even opposing
>   opinions.
> * Identify duplicate or overlapping thoughts.
> * Tolerate ambiguity and/or uncertainty in both language and concepts.

Impact

When Present . . .
> * A greater number of peripheral ideas are actually considered by the
>   group.
> * The merger of opposing thoughts begins a process of negotiation and
>   compromise.
> * Extends an open invitation for the consideration of dissimilar view-
>   points.
> * Transforms raw data into more usable information.

When Absent . . .
> * Attempts at intermingling ideas become bogged down in detail.
> * Questions or options are often ignored when group members are
>   unwilling to entertain alternative opinions.
> * Conflicting statements are easily escalated into widespread
>   arguments.
> * Without a periodic blending, concepts appear disjointed and seem to
>   lack continuity.

Intuitive

Integrate - To skillfully and effectively join separate concepts into a
larger whole.

Requirements

   * Construct a framework within which concepts can be maneuvered.
   * Identify overall patterns or trends across Participants' contributions.
   * Connect thoughts without losing or sacrificing the substance of
     either.
   * Maintain the goal of idea development by using Participant input as
     conceptual building blocks.

Impact

When Present . . .
   * Creates a greater sense of unity among members.
   * Allows Participants to experience the direct impact of their ideas on
     others' thoughts.
   * Demonstrates to Participants how dramatically different combinations
     of ideas can affect an outcome.
   * Provides continuity to the thought process and creates a heightened
     sense of member involvement.

When Absent . . .
   * Following ideas along separate lines often leads to group tunnel
     vision.
   * Loose or incomplete linkage among concepts renders them less
     effective.
   * Fosters an atmosphere of competitiveness rather than cooperation.
   * Concentration and energy for each member is diverted from positive
     group input to individual tracking of conceptual development.

SENSITIVITY

The ability to read, interpret, and eventually anticipate Participant responses is key to successful facilitating. There are two contexts in which this ability is particularly crucial. 1) Establishing common or compatible perspectives; and 2) Actively supporting risk taking during the process.

These contexts require a sensitivity from the Facilitator, as well as the Participants. An environment must be developed and sustained where both individual and group vulnerability can be cultivated. This demands a delicate balance between nurturing emotional states and stimulating new thought patterns.

PERSPECTIVE

There is information that can help the Facilitator achieve this "balance." As an example, Participants have difficulty "connecting" with someone who has no knowledge of their organization. The Facilitator can best serve the group's needs by securing at least a skeletal notion of the organization's structure, culture, and personnel. This information assists the Facilitator in aligning Producer/Participant expectations, and provides a primary bridge to a relationship with group members.

The key question becomes: How much and what kind of information does the Facilitator really need? Interestingly enough, there are usually contradictory viewpoints between a novice Facilitator and a more experienced one. The former is likely to prefer more detailed, hard documentation (structure) and little cultural or emotional input. This normally stems from a greater need for more tangible, clear-cut data. Later in their careers, more experienced Facilitators often prefer minimal or brief "structure" information. Rather, they tend to focus on whatever is available about group members and their psychological/emotional status with regard to each other, the organization, and the discussion topic.

It is important to note that any information given to the Facilitator should be used for reference only. Since impartiality is imperative, making judgments based on data alone may well discredit the Facilitator and destroy or at least considerably slow down the receptive process.

Moving from the known (tangible background information) to the unknown (more illusive, intuitive information) can be used by the Facilitator to construct a comfortability bridge for Participants. Interaction levels can be established earlier in the process and risk taking usually begins more quickly.

RISK TAKING

The facilitative process is a natural environment for risk taking. Opinions, commentaries, intuitive hunches, observations, and suggestions are all subject to a certain amount of risk. We can never be entirely certain how others will respond to our input. An individual may be especially apprehensive if they have had prior negative experiences with participation. As a result, the Facilitator is relied on for encouragement and support.

Perhaps the most common application of risk taking occurs as options are developed. Under such circumstances, there is an absolute need for reciprocal respect. The Facilitator not only sets the tone for this level of idea sharing, but monitors each exchange for continued accuracy and mutual understanding.

In a similar vein, there is vulnerability whenever emotions enter the discussion. The Facilitator's sensitivity to these emotional states is critical. If Participant feelings are ignored, there may be an increase in their intensity (anger or frustration), or there may be complete silence (withdrawal). If Participant feelings are improperly encouraged, there could be an explosive reaction, seriously disrupting the process or altering its outcome.

Ideas should be encouraged by the Facilitator, and feelings should be acknowledged (recognized without bias). The Facilitator must constantly and carefully balance individual with group needs. Ultimately, a conducive environment for risk taking is one in which Participants feel free to develop ideas without ridicule, and express emotions without regret.

SYNERGY

An enormous amount of energy is exchanged during facilitation. This collective group exchange generates a force or synergy that is greater than the sum of its parts. Mental concentration, physical expression, emotional pitch, and spiritual commitment form an atmosphere capable of conducting both positive and negative energy levels. One of the most important functions of the Facilitator is to diffuse the negative, while intensifying the positive. This begins with an understanding of energy transference.

POWER EXCHANGE

"If you can't see it, it isn't there," is a quotation often said, yet seldom relevant. It is particularly misleading when used to describe energy. In facilitation, it would be more accurate to say, "If you see it, it's probably too late."

First and foremost, energy is something <u>felt</u>. It is sensed, experienced, and intuited. In general, it may be used by the Facilitator for two purposes: 1) To provide an indication of the group's overall attitude and any interpersonal relationships; and 2) To persuade, deflect, or influence the members' emotional and psychological states.

Sensing the level and polarity of the group's energy provides the Facilitator with much needed advanced information. Are they Cold? Warm? Excited? Tired? Skeptical? Angry? Apprehensive? The list of possibilities is almost endless and <u>any</u> insight is certainly better than no insight.

Additionally, energy is not stagnant. It is constantly moving and shifting to form new bonds and new intensities. With experience and practice, these shifts can be affected. It is the same principle as a one-on-one encounter.

Imagine feeling very angry about something that has just happened to you. To collect your thoughts, you stop at a restaurant for lunch. Unfortunately, your emotions are "on the surface," and in a short time, it is likely that the demeanor of those serving you will seem a little more edgy, appear slightly more irritated, and become progressively more negative. Our own levels of energy can have a powerful impact on those around us. Nowhere else can this be so enlightening or so devastating than in the facilitation process.

EXTENSION TO THE OUTSIDE

The Facilitator orchestrates and interweaves the thoughts, feelings, and strengths of individual group members into a synergistic decision-making team. Its influence far exceeds the boundaries of the initial group process. Mutual respect for one another's ideas and expertise bonds them together to form an invisible strength of purpose.

This synergy functions as a catalyst for solid leadership and resourcefulness in problem solving both in and outside the group. Within the group, positive energy exchange challenges and heightens creativity. Outside the immediate group, members often seek out one another for specialized tasks and projects. In addition, the proper use of synergy acts as an example of productive team development and an overall positive corporate culture.

CHAPTER SUMMARY

The breakdown of skills discussed in this chapter provides an insight to the complexity and the "art" of effective Facilitation. To possess each of the skills is not enough. The timing, amount, and blending are of equal importance. Further, the Facilitator's efforts must be infused with a visible interest in increasing group potential.

Sensitivity, therefore, to any message, verbal or nonverbal, is a necessity for Facilitators. Any information is useful, but some pieces are of particular importance. An understanding of the culture of the organization, the history of the group, and the attitudes and expectations of its members are indispensable. With this information, the Facilitator can more effectively manage the group's interactional and decision-making environment.

Facilitators' skills and sensitivity produce an invisible link between themselves and group members. This link provides the atmosphere necessary to create a synergistic state within which the group operates. It is a powerful communication tool that can maximize group performance.

V. THE EXPRESSION
(Matrix)

DESIGN

An often overlooked aspect of Facilitation is the initial selection process. Producers or their consultants must choose who will facilitate and who will participate in the sessions. Although this may appear to be relatively simple, a closer look shows a far more complex interaction among selection criteria and desired outcomes.

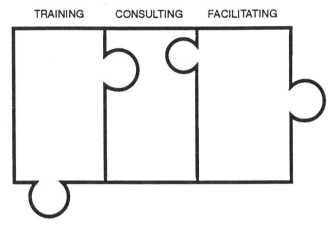

As we stated earlier, Trainers, Consultants, and Facilitators are usually placed in a single category in terms of skills and abilities. When outcomes differ from expectations, Producers believe that they have misjudged the Provider's personality and/or background.

While these may be valid factors, the real issue is: What skills were needed for the specific task? Another way to state the question would be: Were the skills and experience of the Provider properly matched to the needs of the Participants and the task?

It is no surprise that confusion occurs in selection, since identifying and separating skills by "task to be accomplished" is not often considered. To unravel this confusion, we have developed an easy-to-use matrix.

DESCRIPTION

This Selection Matrix is designed to compare and contrast the application of Training, Consulting, and Facilitating. An examination of all potential variables would be impossible. Identified below, therefore, are eight selection criteria which serve as parameters for the matrix.

We believe these criteria have the greatest direct impact on the selection process. They are organized under four categorical headings: Organization; Task; Provider; Participant.

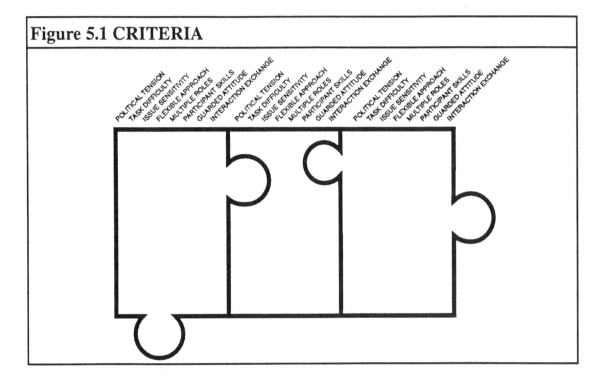

Figure 5.1 CRITERIA

Operational Guidelines

Organization

Political Tension - An organizational climate reflects the pervasive belief or mood of those within it.

* What is the current state of the organization's psychological and emotional environment?
* Is dissatisfaction or unrest present among its members?
* Are power and rank used for personal rather than organizational gain?

Task

Task Difficulty - Any desired outcome is comprised of a series of
simple to complex tasks.

* What is the highest level of difficulty among the required
tasks?
* How much mental and/or emotional effort will any one of
these tasks demand?
* Will any part of these tasks require outside/additional
expertise?

Issue Sensitivity - Certain issues may be politically, psychologically,
or emotionally charged.

* Will a decision affect a particular individual or group?
* Is there a noticeable, emotional reaction to certain issues?
* Is there known historical baggage associated with the issue?

Provider

Flexible Approach - Sessions may be more or less structured,
according to specific task and issue
requirements.

* Should an agenda be used?
* Have Participants traditionally worked in a structured
environment?
* Are time constraints an issue?

Multiple Roles - The Provider is required to assume the responsibility
for more than a single task.

* Is this person expected to select session Participants?
* Are any written reports required?
* Is it necessary that session data be used for other purposes or
presented in other settings?

Participant Skills - A determination must be made as to the competency level of each group member to fully engage themselves in the process.

* Are Participants accustomed to working in a group setting?
* How experienced are Participants with problem-solving techniques?
* Can they clearly articulate ideas and opinions?

Guarded Attitude - Individuals may be apprehensive or suspicious regarding session content, process, or outcome.

* Do the Participants tend to mask their true opinions?
* Do the Participants distrust the session's stated purpose?
* How frequently do those involved react in a defensive manner?

Interaction Exchange - Participation levels can vary from one task to another.

* Will group exercises be part of the process?
* Is any part of the process likely to result in disagreement or conflict?
* Is a high level of interaction required to produce the desired outcome?

In addition to the eight criteria, we have measured their impact by indicating a level of intensity:

66 - 100%   High

33 - 65%   Moderate

0 - 32%   Low

Figure 5.2 SELECTION MATRIX

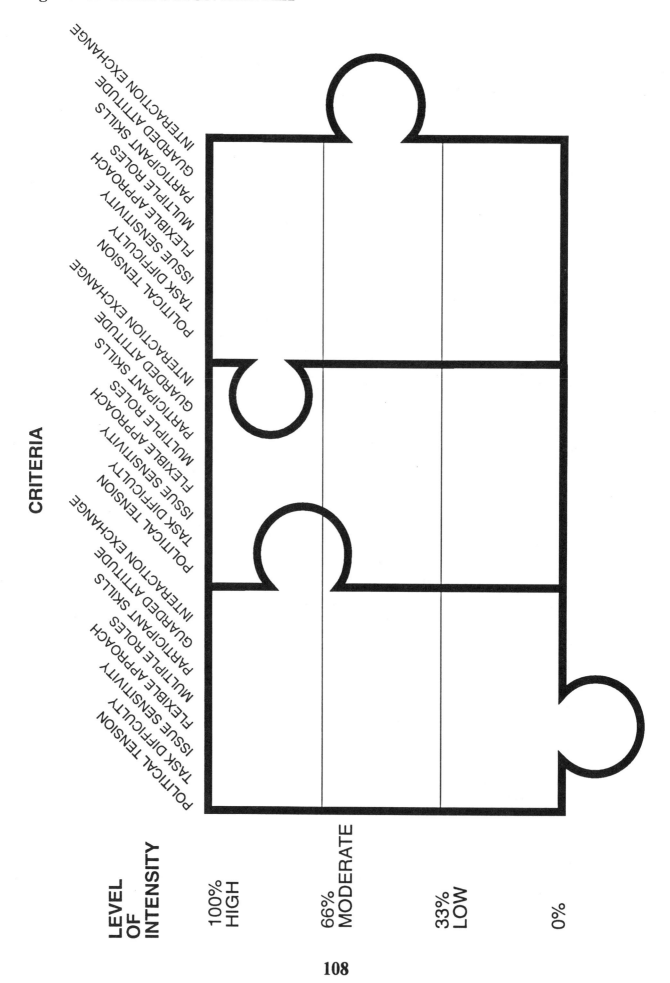

CRITERIA

POLITICAL TENSION
TASK DIFFICULTY
ISSUE SENSITIVITY
FLEXIBLE APPROACH
MULTIPLE ROLES
PARTICIPANT SKILLS
GUARDED ATTITUDE
INTERACTION EXCHANGE

POLITICAL TENSION
TASK DIFFICULTY
ISSUE SENSITIVITY
FLEXIBLE APPROACH
MULTIPLE ROLES
PARTICIPANT SKILLS
GUARDED ATTITUDE
INTERACTION EXCHANGE

POLITICAL TENSION
TASK DIFFICULTY
ISSUE SENSITIVITY
FLEXIBLE APPROACH
MULTIPLE ROLES
PARTICIPANT SKILLS
GUARDED ATTITUDE
INTERACTION EXCHANGE

LEVEL
OF
INTENSITY

100%
HIGH

66%
MODERATE

33%
LOW

0%

As tasks are analyzed, the above criteria are graphed (High, Moderate, Low), according to each one's probable impact. If the majority of criteria fall in a Low-level intensity, the task is probably best suited for Training. If the majority of criteria fall in a Moderate-level intensity, the task is likely suitable for Consulting. Finally, if the criteria appear in a High-level intensity, it is suggested that the Producer seek a Facilitator. Following are three examples in which these criteria are used to determine the optimal match between Provider and task.

DIRECTION

SITUATION 1

A retail photo-copy business has prepared new invoicing procedures. All service area employees need to understand the requirements.

CRITERIA

Political Tension
Although there is some dissatisfaction with the central office, this particular branch has a relaxed and cooperative atmosphere.

Task Difficulty
These new procedures will require the employees to develop new habits. Although this will necessitate time, it is not anticipated to cause undo physical or mental stress.

Issue Sensitivity
Among those employees with the most years of service, there is some, but not dramatic resistance to the changes. In addition, although a few individuals will have added tasks, the overall balance of responsibilities will be improved.

Flexible Approach
The information can be delivered in a direct manner. Group scheduling should be staggered so that each service shift can be accommodated during working hours.

Multiple Roles
The Participants are predetermined, and although the session will likely be repeated three or four times, it will be the same material for each occasion.

Participant Skills
In general, the task involves information dissemination. The discussion process, therefore, is not anticipated to be demanding. A minimal level of learning skills would be expected.

Guarded Attitude
As stated before, some employees may be initially resistant to the changes. Still, there is a history of periodic procedural changes in the company, with no apparent long-term frustration or resentment.

Interaction Exchange
There may be Participant discussion concerning logistics, but no decision making is required.

Figure 5.3 SITUATION 1

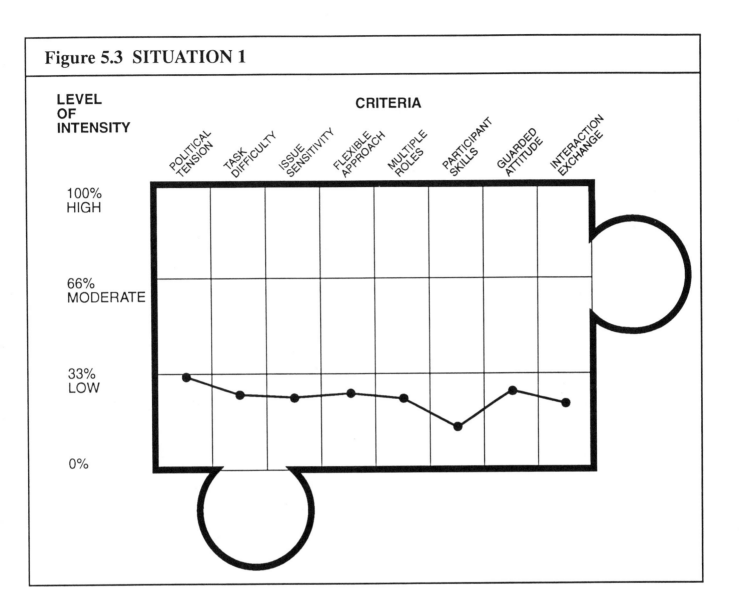

SITUATION 2

The Chief Executive Officer of a manufacturing firm knows friction exists between the line and staff departments. However, she is too close to the situation to identify the reason(s) for it.

CRITERIA

Political Tension

An example of the comments coming from members of the line departments is: Who is really in charge - - the support department or the administration? Who are the decision makers? Although there seems to be some role confusion, there is an overall spirit of cooperation.

Task Difficulty

Individual departments should be queried to investigate problems and situations. Are there any trends? Do all the problems lead to the same person? Is there only one basic problem? It will need to be determined whether the solution will require long-term planning and implementation or a short-term, quick response.

Issue Sensitivity

No particular issue seems to stand out. Several people from both the line and staff departments tend to be extremely vocal on several issues.

Flexible Approach

Interviews or sessions with all concerned may be moderately structured. Trust between the Provider and Participants must be established, since probing for information will be essential to reach root causes.

Multiple Roles

This situation calls for the Provider to gain an understanding of the work flow in each department, develop and maintain a solid rapport with those involved, and provide alternative solutions to the administration in both oral and written form.

Participant Skills

The employees involved have a minimal amount of group problem-solving experience. They are used to coming together only for one-way informational meetings.

Guarded Attitudes

Some amount of employee frustration is evident, but the overall focus is still directed toward the company's advancement.

Interaction Exchange

Breaking down communication barriers between various departments is critical. Small group meetings between departments should open the door to greater understanding and empathy for each others' situations. In addition, information pathways throughout the company must be improved.

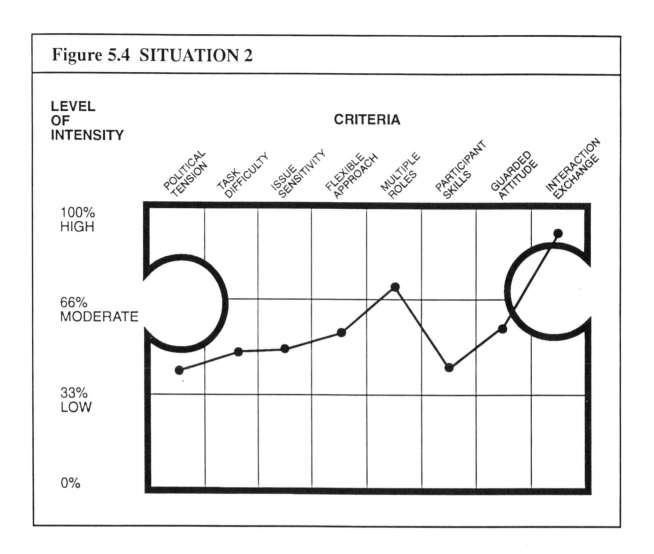

Figure 5.4 SITUATION 2

LEVEL
OF
INTENSITY

CRITERIA

POLITICAL
TENSION

TASK
DIFFICULTY

ISSUE
SENSITIVITY

FLEXIBLE
APPROACH

MULTIPLE
ROLES

PARTICIPANT
SKILLS

GUARDED
ATTITUDE

INTERACTION
EXCHANGE

100%
HIGH

66%
MODERATE

33%
LOW

0%

SITUATION 3

A community agency is planning how their funds will be allocated over the next fifteen years. They attempted a similar session three years ago with unfavorable results.

CRITERIA

Political Tension

There is a fair amount of disagreement over where and to whom the funds should be allocated. At least four of the agency's thirteen members have developed isolated pockets of support in the community. Each of these sources is competing for funds.

Task Difficulty

Given the political nature of the decisions, the Participants should be interviewed prior to the session. In addition, previous allocations should be reviewed, and the results may be surveyed. The session itself should yield both an oral report and a written analysis.

Issue Sensitivity

Since the previous session was not successful, there is a great deal of apprehension and skepticism among the members. This has the potential, therefore, of creating an atmosphere of defensiveness and/or hostility.

Flexible Approach

How the Participants will respond to another attempt at group problem solving is uncertain. The session leader, therefore, will need to be flexible in working through any predetermined agenda items.

Multiple Roles

The task itself has several subcomponents. As such, the session organizer must also collect, interpret and analyze the information.

Participant Skills	Those involved are accustomed to participating in internal and external group problem-solving situations. They are generally adept at presenting their ideas in an efficient and persuasive manner.
Guarded Attitude	There is a pervasive assumption that funds will be allocated only to those individuals holding, or able to influence, the greatest political clout. This belief hinders creativity, although agency members openly state that they would like to see a resolution to the allocation issue.
Interaction Exchange	Historically, the Participants have taken strong stands on their own positions. Agreement or solutions, therefore, may be difficult. A case must be built to focus their efforts on the greater good for the overall community.

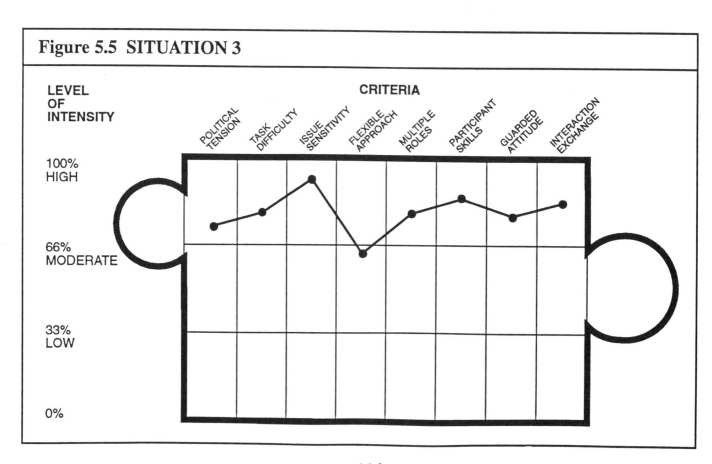

Figure 5.5 SITUATION 3

As we indicated before, when most points fall in the low range, a Trainer would likely fit the needs. When the majority appear mid-range, the needs would better be matched to a Consultant. If most points are positioned in the high range, a Facilitator would be most appropriated.

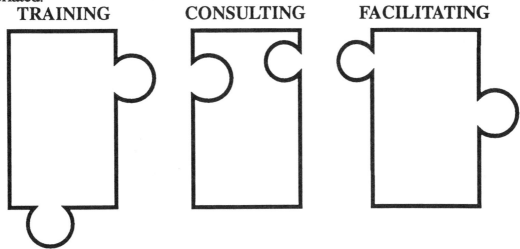

	Brainstorming	Problem Solving	Group Consensus
EXAMPLES OF OUTCOMES	Team-Building Techniques	Strategic Planning	Decision Making
	Information Dissemination	Decision Making	Team Development
	Orientations	Crisis Intervention	Issue Analysis
	Technical Skills	Negotiation	Strategic Planning
	Human Skills	Conflict Resolution	Negotiation
			Conflict
			Resolution
PROBABLE CHOICE	**TRAINER**	**CONSULTANT**	**FACILITATOR**
	Transfer of Knowledge	Provide Direction for Problem Resolution	Assist in Intra/Intergroup Communication

JUDGMENT CALLS

Introduction

The above examples demonstrate how the model can assist in matching "type of person needed" to "task to be accomplished." Accurately matching the two is, in many cases, a judgment call.

To base those judgement calls only on "gut feelings" or "instinct" is unnecessary and inappropriate. Rather, prior selection choices and/or tools like the model above can improve the odds of a more productive decision.

Placement

There is a general guideline for selecting a High, Moderate, or Low level of intensity for each criterion. Criteria should be scaled in their intensity by what is relative to that particular group or organization. In other words, the criterion "Political Tension" for the city's major hotel may be "Moderate" when compared to its neighboring manufacturing plant. For the hotel, however, it is unusually strained. The most appropriate placement, therefore, would be "High" intensity.

With the scaling, a higher rating indicates a conservative perspective, while a lower rating indicates a more risky one. If in doubt, err on the High level of intensity. The individual you then hire should be able to properly adjust to a Low level of intensity if necessary. It also creates a "safety margin" in case the situation should evolve into something more sensitive and/or volatile.

Analysis

Once an intensity for each criterion is chosen, the chart may be interpreted. Two considerations are of particular importance to this analysis. First, high "spikes" on the graph indicate criterion extremes. This should be examined carefully, since even one spike may be sufficient to warrant a shift in choice between Trainer, Consultant, or Facilitator.

Second, "Political Tension," "Issue Sensitivity," and "Guarded Attitude," produce the greatest emotional impact. A High intensity mark for any one of them, therefore, would indicate a correspondingly high potential for hostility.

Evaluation

Broad assumptions about why certain Providers used in the past were successes or failures need not be a mere "gut" reaction. Producers can check their selection accuracy by a more methodical review of past experiences. Questions might include:

* Did each match secure a productive outcome?
* Which criteria outlined in the model seem to have caused the most difficulty?
* How could these difficulties be eliminated or at least minimized in the future?

Producers should develop their own short list of evaluation questions like the ones listed above. The questions, of course, should relate directly to the needs of their organization.

One additional comment: Be careful not to confuse "expected" with "productive." Producers and/or Participants may feel dissatisfied with a session merely because they held different expectations, or believed in a predetermined outcome. Remember, productivity does not necessarily equal speed, bias, or feelings of satisfaction. Be as thorough as possible in an assessment of the Provider-Task matching.

Players

The dynamics of any group are a direct reflection of the composition of individual members and their reactions, responses, and interactions with one another. In addition, the Facilitator provides the spark to ignite and maintain the group's energy for the duration of the session(s).

An opportunity to custom design a problem-solving or decision-making group may be absent. Oftentimes, Participants are included because they are already members of an existing work unit (department, division, or committee). When group composition is optional, however, a greater balance of personality matching and diversity can be achieved. For example, Participants may be selected, in part, on their commitment to both the process and the group itself. In addition, representative input from all impacted areas should be obtained if at all possible.

Although it is not mandatory, it is often helpful to have a variety of personality types and levels of knowledge among group members. This lends depth and breadth to the discussion. Issue agreement/disagreement is not a prerequisite for group membership. In fact, research indicates that diversity is a strong deterrent to Groupthink. [1]

For the Provider (Facilitator), skill competency is vital. Closely linked is a consideration of personality and general style. Experienced Facilitators should be able to adjust to the group's characteristics and style of interaction.

Still, some groups may be highly verbal, others unexpectedly quiet. Some are more social and informal, others more formal and rigid. Despite the Facilitator's fluency in translating and managing these differences, there are certain matches that will help or hinder the adjustment process. A sensitivity to divergence of style between the Participants and the Facilitator is recommended.

Even extreme differences, however, do not automatically mean difficulty or rejection for the Facilitator. What it should signal is the need for a second look. There are Facilitators who can and do adapt exceptionally well to virtually any group or surrounding circumstances.

---

[1] Janis,I.L, *Groupthink*, Second Edition, (Boston,MA: Houghton Mifflin Company, 1983).
   Miller, W.C.,*The Creative Edge: Fostering Innovation Where You Work* (Reading,MA: Addison Wesley Publishing Company, Inc., 1987).
   Gouran,D.S., *Making Decisions in Groups: Choices and Consequences* (Glenview,IL: Scott Foresman & Co., 1982).

Finally, as Facilitator selection is reviewed, remember the primary criterion centers on perceived and/or actual objectivity. Ask:

* Does the Facilitator have experience dealing with similar groups?

* Are there any apparent vested interests in the outcome of the session?

* Are the Facilitator's feelings about the topic likely to impact the guidance of the group?

* What is your overall impression of objectivity when interacting with this individual?

Common sense, mixed with properly phrased questions will usually serve the decision maker of this dilemma better than set rules.

DEVELOPMENT

The impact of Facilitation is varied in both time and scope. Some influences are immediate, others longer term. We have selected eight commonly reported effects of the facilitative process and its outcomes. Increased awareness of these effects and their potential positive and negative impact can help the Facilitator anticipate and design needed strategies and interventions.

Figure 5.6 PROCESS EFFECTS		
	Positive	**Negative**
Learning Curve	The more often individuals participate in a group process, the more comfortable they are with their own vulnerability and the more accomplished they will become at designated tasks.	Learning any new skill can be demanding. The Facilitator may see resistance, frustration, mistrust, or even anger displayed during the early stages.
Issue Discovery	Frequently, issues surface during sessions that provide sensitive or cause/effect information useful and/or essential to outcomes.	Previously hidden or unknown issues often surface during a facilitated process. Members may be reluctant to address or even acknowledge them.
Team Building	Not only will the members develop as a group, but individuals should become less hesitant concerning involvement in other teams and/or task forces.	As in all relationships, groups progress through phases. Earlier stages may include behaviors such as withdrawal, conflict with one another, or even rejection of the Facilitator.
Decision Making	A wider range and a more thorough exploration of alternatives may be developed. This is a pattern that should reinforce itself continuously.	Shallow decisions will become more evident and unacceptable to Participants. This may result in defensiveness, anger, or lowered self-confidence.

Figure 5.7 OUTCOME EFFECTS

	Positive	Negative
Premature Closings	There seems to be an immediate gratification for group members in almost any type of conclusion. Arriving at closure can provide satisfaction and a sense of accomplishment.	When the process is cut short merely to attain an "end," issues are not thoroughly discussed. Quality is often sacrificed. Inevitably, these same issues will re-emerge, often with more serious implications.
Unexpected Conclusions	Although the initial session goal is reached, the process may also produce additional outcomes. Decisions may then be made to pursue alternative concerns or examine a wider range of isolated issues.	The "unexpected" is disconcerting to some people. A discussion of additional or peripheral concerns may prompt the belief that the session focus has been distorted or abandoned. Awareness of this can prepare the Facilitator for group skepticism and a temporary withdrawal of trust.
Future Direction/ Action	Whatever the outcome, there should be some type of indication that an agreement has been attained (even if the decision is to continue discussion). Forward motion is imperative for progress.	Members do not always define or accept action in the same manner. Some take more time to think through the ramifications. In addition, some members will not acknowledge discussion and planning as action steps, and may become frustrated with what they perceive to be slow or absent progress.
Individual Abilities	This provides the impetus for individual team members to call on one another outside the process environment. The purpose is to draw on all members' ideas and expertise.	Group intraction quickly identifies individuals who have fewer skills and/or are less committed to the process. This then, will usually require some type of deliberate action by the Facilitator or other Participants.

123

CHAPTER SUMMARY

Producers should take a hard look at the initial selection process. This chapter is designed to aid them in arriving at a proper match between the task and the individual they wish to use. The necessity to thoroughly identify issues and choose the most appropriately skilled person is quite clear. Further, when the implications of an incorrect choice are considered, the selection process becomes critical.

That choice, however, is complex. Too often, both the skills and the applications of Training, Consulting, and Facilitating are treated as though they were completely interchangeable. The eight criteria identified in this chapter are meant to serve as guidelines in alleviating this confusion.

Three situational examples demonstrate how the circumstances of any task can be graphed to give a visual picture of its overall needs. Special considerations and marginal "judgment calls" are then used to help make the final determination as to the type of person best suited for the task.

If a Facilitator is selected, the group's composition will also affect the dynamics, synergy, and interactional patterns during such a process. Composition itself may be optional. This, of course, would provide both the Producer and the Facilitator with maximum flexibility. More often than not, however, group membership is determined by task, work department, or unit association.

In either case, the Facilitator's personal style and the expected "group personality" should be at least informally compared for compatibility. Although a perfect "fit" is by no means a requirement, comparisons are of particular importance for inexperienced Facilitators, since their ability to adjust to extreme groups is usually limited.

Finally, possible process and outcome effects of facilitation are reviewed. It is intended that an awareness of how these impact individual members, as well as the group itself, will provide insights to the Producer, and increased confidence for the Facilitator.

VI. THE EDGE
(Payoff)

The book's goal is to establish a concrete foundation for a fledgling profession that is just beginning to come into its own. We have reviewed the historical mixing of other professions into something called *facilitation*, and have attempted to sort out the confusion caused by this blending. In general, the existing confusion has stunted the progress of facilitation's use as a powerful, multi-purpose communication tool.

The primary strength of this tool is in its flexibility and depth. It can be adapted easily to a variety of tasks in a wide range of settings. The facilitation process seeks to flesh out a discussion to its fullest. Ideas are generated and developed, emotional issues are discussed, and alternatives are offered and evaluated, thereby maximizing input and decision-making potential.

The "depth" of facilitation usually depends on the Provider's (Facilitator's) ability to "work" the group. That is, the Facilitator must create and maintain a psychological and physical environment conducive to Participants by influencing their willingness to share information and ideas. In order to provide that support, those facilitating must possess not only informative and interpretive skills, but intuitive abilities as well. Utilizing these skills beyond what is needed for training or consulting should result in a more coordinated synergy among Participants.

SYNOPSIS

WORKING FOUNDATION

We have provided what we believe to be a basic premise for the understanding and development of facilitation. As a hybrid of skill and art, it is multifaceted in both mastery and application.

We also believe that, as with any learning process, repetition can fine tune an individual's ability to facilitate. Application results in experience, and reviewed experience fosters more effective application.

RELATED TERMINOLOGY

Throughout the book, Training and Consulting have been used as direct points to compare and contrast. We realize, however, that these are not the only labels closely associated with facilitation.

Below are six additional terms commonly considered to be related to this tool. Although each term <u>does</u> contain elements of facilitation, some are being used as fully interchangeable descriptors. Confusion often results, and facilitation itself simply becomes a "catch-all" definition. This confusion can be lessened, however, by identifying these terms along a continuum of commonalty with the facilitation process.

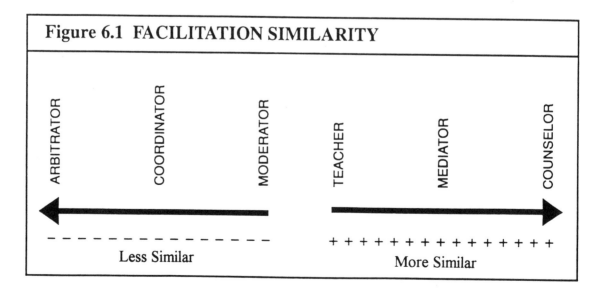

Figure 6.1 FACILITATION SIMILARITY

A further explanation is provided below. It lists the dictionary definition[1] of each term followed by its similarities to/differences from facilitation.

Arbitrator	"An impartial person chosen to decide/settle a dispute between parties."
	The facilitative role is used to help others during their decision-making process. In and of itself, however, it is not intended to decide outcomes or make final determinations.
Coordinator	"To put in the same order or rank/to bring into a common action, movement, or condition. To cause to work together efficiently."
	This role almost exclusively addresses the logistics of a given situation. The focus of facilitation, however, is on process not procedure.
Moderator	"One who presides over an assembly/a presiding officer."
	It is common that someone will request a Facilitator for a meeting, when what they actually require is a moderator. There is a way to distinguish these choices. Translation, summarization, and interpretation needs are best served by a Facilitator. On the other hand, a need to introduce and bridge, regulate conversation, and monitor time constraints suggests the use of a moderator.

---

[1] *Oxford American Dictionary* (New York, NY: Oxford University Press. 1980) *Websters New Collegiate Dictionary* (Springfield, MA: G&G Merriam Co., 1977).

| **Teacher** | "To instruct/to seek to make known and accepted." |
| | |

In general, teaching and training are similar, and both involve a dissemination of information, along with the development of knowledge. In addition, some facilitative skills are also used in the teaching process.

Mediator   "To act as negotiator or peacemaker between opposing sides in a dispute/to intervene between conflicting parties so as to promote reconciliation, settlement, or compromise."

A Facilitator functions more as a guide through conflict resolution, than as an actual intermediary. Any intervention by a mediator, however, usually requires the use of facilitative skills.

Counselor   "To give advice/providing consultation/professional guidance of the individual by utilizing psychological methods."

The term "counseling" is perhaps the closest to facilitation. Many, if not most of the skills are shared by both roles. Each are intended to help guide individuals through a decision-making process. One important caveat, however, is to make certain the Facilitator's background is not limited to one-on-one counseling, but is well supported by organizational systems experience.

Manager and **Leader** are two additional terms associated almost synonomously with facilitation. Each implies a particular function and/or position in the organization. Too often, however, it is presumed that these individuals possess a thorough knowledge and understanding of facilitation. Unfortunately, the skill sets for each of these professional roles do not necessarily overlap. There is, therefore, no current reliable method to predict a correlation between organizational position and facilitation skills.

SIGNIFICANCE

Since facilitation is used as a supplement, its advantages are not always clearly identified. Below are samplings of both direct and indirect benefits from this underutilized tool.

The process of facilitation provides a communication environment where a freer exchange of information and ideas can occur. Participants gain confidence in their ability to convey ideas, perspectives, and concerns to other group members with less fear of ridicule, rejection, or retaliation. This more honest interaction paves the way for a better understanding and respect of one anothers' viewpoints. Generally, individual commitment to the end results of such a session is stronger and longer lasting.

Decisions are made continuously in any organizational setting. The quality of those decisions is enhanced by the facilitative process in several ways. First, there is greater freedom of expression to field new ideas and expand the number of alternatives. Second, it provides insight to gauge the breadth and depth of individual group member's ability to:

      1) Think in the abstract;

      2) Grasp both the macro and micro perspectives of issues;

      3) Understand, appreciate, and utilize group synergy to reach
         productive conclusions.

SCOPE OF IMPACT

There are oftentimes far-reaching implications that stem from a facilitative process. Individuals and groups are usually the most directly affected. Nevertheless, departments, the organization as a whole, and even those outside the organization (clients/customers, suppliers, competitors, regulatory agencies, etc.) are impacted by the process and its outcomes.

Individuals

There is less fear of vulnerability and the feeling of control over their own work life increases. As a result, they develop confidence in their ability to share ideas and solve problems.

Group

Peers learn more about the way in which each member thinks. This opens the door for honest communication. Problems become challenges, and are no longer approached with dread. Finally, as members gain experience, a greater understanding of the power and productiveness of group synergism generally evolves.

Department

Communication gaps among departments are diminished and in some cases, entirely eliminated. Problems are then shared and resolved, rather than viewed as points of blame. In addition, cross-training among departments is easier to initiate and implement.

Organization

The overall atmosphere is more stimulating and pleasant. Employees are more committed to organizational goals, since they play an active role in planning and decision making. There is less fear of change, and a greater anticipation of future progress. Further, turnover diminishes due to higher employee job satisfaction.

External Environment

The organization is seen as a role model for others seeking to embrace a participative management culture. After all, it is easier and more satisfying to interact with a company whose employees work together as a team. The timeliness and quality of information provided demonstrate a team knowledge of the problem at hand, while maintaining a focus on the big picture.

SEED

Although *facilitation* has become a commonly used term in today's business community, its meaning is unclear. Definitions vary depending on the background of those queried. In addition, if asked what skills and expertise are required to conduct such a process, these same people might have difficulty responding. If they did answer, it is likely that their responses would be as different from one another as their backgrounds.

As a result, facilitation is not always applied appropriately and/or to its maximum potential. Properly used, it can be a powerful developer of individuals, groups, or teams. The key to its influence lies in the Facilitator's ability to use the process; that is, understand all of its facets and amplify its activities to the fullest.

There are no current glossaries or rule manuals for facilitation. This book describes, develops, and defines a much needed set of parameters for the widely-used tool. Further, the chapters are designed for multi-targeted markets: Producers (those who select or hire Facilitators); Providers (Facilitators themselves); and Participants.

A quick perusal of facilitation yields a lengthy list of applications.

Figure 6.2 CURRENT STATUS OF FACILITATION

> Brainstorming and Creativity
> Change Management
> Competitive Analyses
> Conferences, Retreats, and Forums
> Conflict Resolution
> Contingency Planning
> Decision Making by Group or Individuals
> Employee Education
> Empowerment
> Goal Setting
> Government Meetings (town, city, state, and public)
> Group Development/Dynamics
> Hiring and Termination
> Individual How-To or Self-Assessment
> Intra- and Inter-Departmental Relations
> Meeting Planning
> Mergers and Acquisitions
> Negotiations
> Participative Management
> Problem Identification
> Reorganization
> Research and Development
> Rightsizing
> Strategic Planning
> Surveys
> Team Building
> Total Quality Management

Facilitation's involvement spans a diverse listing of topics, skills, needs, and techniques. Below, we have described how it might be utilized in four designated areas.

Decision Making

Problem-solving or decision-making groups often stumble through a process or retrace steps while groping for direction. In addition, meetings can be a tremendous waste of time if the Participants are not prepared for their responsibilities.

Group members have their own opinions concerning decisions. Expressing those opinions, translating, interpreting and compromising are all part of the Facilitator's role. Choosing a capable Facilitator can save many wasted hours and may even lower Participant disappointment. Those trained in these skills can help transform a mediocre work group into a productive and effective organizational team. They can create and maintain positive environments for problem solving, and thereby increase the opportunity for effective decision making.

Goal Setting

Regardless of the particular team, individuals enter management groups with varying sets of expectations. An effective Facilitator can go far in aligning expectations and evaluating the self-esteem of group members.

A Facilitator can help clarify the roles and responsibilities of all those involved. Further, by encouraging group participation, the Facilitator can lower individual frustrations while raising overall commitments to organizational goals. These guidelines, in turn, help develop shared goals and provide a basis for understanding and communication.

Participative Management

With the popularity of participatory management comes the realization that employees (group participants) have not moved into this mode of thinking and behaving as easily as was originally anticipated. The tradition of "management thinks - employees do" is a deeply ingrained pattern. Management commitment, sufficient training, and competent facilitation are critical to the process.

There is also the issue of taking proactive steps. Prevention is, after all, just as important as cost reduction. Knowing how to choose qualified and compatible Facilitators can lower the psychological and physical costs of wasted time and group discouragement.

Participant preparation will often determine the group's level of productivity. Discussions can lead to literally right or wrong decisions based on the skill and sensitivity of the Facilitator to draw out possible contributions by group members. Finally, during the process itself, proper facilitation can identify and/or diffuse individual objections before they result in delayed implementation, sabotage, or complete inaction.

Organizational Objectives

The Facilitator can create a positive environment by supporting a bond of trust among group members. This trust allows for idea generation in a non-threatening, non-judgmental atmosphere. As a result, a greater number, and in many cases, more creative ideas are shared.

Using this trust, the Facilitator can coach group members into capable teams committed to organizational rather than individual goals. Perhaps most importantly, a Facilitator can lend the necessary objective viewpoint to the process.

In order to match and surpass competition, teams need to have the skills necessary to constantly question, re-examine issues, and align resources for goal attainment. Facilitation helps identify and analyze the internal and external elements concerning competitors. This group synergy, then, contributes to an environment in which the organizational goals are easier to visualize and attain.

FUTURE GROWTH POTENTIAL

This is what we know: The number of people involved with and impacted by decision making continues to grow. The type and amount of information needed for sound decision making expands on a daily, and sometimes hourly basis. Finally, the process for examining the range of implications at almost any level of decision making is becoming more and more complex.

Given these observations, it is likely that the use of facilitation will only escalate. Even though information technology is and will continue to be extremely powerful, it cannot replace the very human process of idea-exchange and interpretation. Facilitators will be needed to negotiate, participate in mergers and acquisitions, resolve conflicts, focus strategic planning, and develop research and expansion projects. Whenever symbols and meanings must find commonality, there is a need for translation, interpretation, and guidance. The Facilitator acts as an impartial catalyst to this much needed process of communication and decision making.

FEEDBACK

The book's purpose is to clarify facilitation issues and identify required Facilitator skills. In addition, it functions as a quick-reference guide to the various groups of people directly involved in the facilitation process. There are three general groups to whom the book carries the greatest benefit:

> Producers (those responsible for Facilitator selection);
> Providers (the Facilitators themselves); and,
> Participants (group members).

*Those responsible for selecting Facilitators are offered parameters and criteria to assist in standardizing the selection/decision process.

*Facilitators and/or trainers of Facilitators are given an opportunity for enhancing their knowledge and understanding of the process. In addition, they are provided a breakdown of required skill sets. These tools will enable them to make more accurate assessments and assist in honing existing skills.

*Participants are made aware of their roles and responsibilities for group interaction. Additionally, they gain a better perspective of how they, as individuals, directly affect process outcomes.

It is important to remember that either an accomplishment or a disappointment can be the first step in molding an environment to make the next session more productive. Since facilitation's role can be dramatically enhanced by any information gathered, the authors would appreciate hearing from those who read and utilize the book.

Correspondence may be directed to the authors at the following addresses:

A.L. Zimmerman, Ph.D.
Interax® Corporation
4524 So. Michigan
P.O. Box 6610
South Bend, IN 46615

Carol J. Evans, President
Monogram
Organizational Development Co.
13633 Haynes Avenue
P.O. Box 470
Mishawaka, IN 46546